CEO Guide to Doing Business in Middle East: United Arab Emirates, Saudi Arabia, Kuwait, Bahrain and Qatar

By Ade Asefeso MCIPS MBA

Second Edition

ISBN-13: 978-1500102456

ISBN-10: 1500102458

Publisher: AA Global Sourcing Ltd
Website: http://www.aaglobalsourcing.com

Table of Contents

Disclaimer

This publication is designed to provide competent and reliable information regarding the subject matter covered. However, it is sold with the understanding that the author and publisher are not engaged in rendering professional advice. The authors and publishers specifically disclaim any liability that is incurred from the use or application of contents of this book.

If you purchased this book without a cover you should be aware that this book may have been stolen property and reported as "unsold and destroyed" to the publisher. In this case neither the author nor the publisher has received any payment for this "stripped book."

Dedication

To my family and friends who seems to have been sent here to teach me something about who I am supposed to be. They have nurtured me, challenged me, and even opposed me.... But at every juncture has taught me!

This book is dedicated to my lovely boys, Thomas, Michael and Karl. Teaching them to manage their finance will give them the lives they deserve. They have taught me more about life, presence, and energy management than anything I have done in my life.

Part 1: CEO Guide to Doing Business in United Arab Emirates (UAE)

Chapter 1: Introduction

The UAE is situated in the southeast of the Arabian Peninsula on the Persian Gulf, bordering Oman and Saudi Arabia. The UAE is a federation of seven Emirates each with its own Ruler. These are Abu Dhabi, Dubai, Sharjah, Fujairah, Ajman, Ras Al Khaimah and Umm Al Quwain. The capital and second largest city is Abu Dhabi, which is also the country's centre of political, industrial and cultural activities.

Since its formation in 1971, the UAE has undergone a period of rapid and wide ranging economic and social development and within 40 years, Dubai is considered the regional hub for business in the Middle East and beyond.

Key facts about Dubai
1. Dubai is regarded as a regional hub.
2. No taxation on personal income and capital gains.
3. English is widely spoken and accepted as business language.
4. Entry route to other GCC countries.
5. UAE is the UK's largest export market in the region.
6. Majority of UAE population are expatriates with 120,000 UK residents.

Opportunities in UAE

The UAE offers major business opportunities in the Middle East with the following priority sectors identified by the federal government;
1. Energy
2. Travel and tourism
3. Financial services
4. Professional services
5. Transport and logistics services
6. Construction
7. Education and healthcare

Looking at this in connection with economic data and fiscal stimulus initiatives, we judge that the main opportunities will be in oil and gas, energy, construction, mass transport, security, health and education.

In 2010 The United Arab Emirates (UAE) was the UK's largest export market in the Middle East and North Africa. It is the UK's 16th largest export of goods market at around £3.9 billion and is designated as one of the UK Trade & Investment High Growth Markets.

In 2010, UK exports to the UAE were £3,891 million which represents an increase of 9% on the same period in 2009. UK Imports were £1,669 million representing an increase of 47% on the same period in 2009. But the UAE remains the UK's biggest export market in the region, and the 16th overall.

British goods cover a wide spectrum of sectors such as telecommunications, power generating machinery and equipment, electrical goods, transport, office machinery, interior and retail goods and non-metallic mineral manufacture. A significant proportion of imports are re-exported to Saudi Arabia and Iran.

Chapter 2: United Arab Emirates Economic Overview

The UAE promotes a liberal business environment and has a standard of living that continues to attract expatriates from around the world. The UAE is looking to diversity its economy away from a reliance on oil and gas. The global economic downturn will reduce growth in the UAE from its historic recent highs of over 10%. The sectors most likely to be affected are construction, real estate and financial services.

In order to stimulate the economy and keep strategically important infrastructure projects on track, Dubai announced a 42% increase in public spending in 2009 to Dhs37.7 billion. This represents a fiscal deficit of Dhs4.2 billion. 45% of spending was been set aside for infrastructure and public transport development a 33% increase on 2008. 22% of the Dubai budget is allocated for social spending including education and health with a further 19% on security, borders and the judiciary.

The long term economic outlook for the UAE is positive. Abu Dhabi's oil and gas driven wealth underpins economic development throughout the UAE. Abu Dhabi has proven oil reserves for 100 years and revenues from that sector are projected to be some US$29,117 billion.

The UAE owns some of the world's biggest investment funds, including the biggest, ADIA, which has estimated reserves of between US$500-900 billion.

Population

According to latest population estimates by the National Bureau of Statistics on 31 March 2011, the UAE's population has grown exponentially to 8.26 million in mid-2010, a growth of 64.5% in four years, as strong economic growth attracted workers from all over the world.

Chapter 3: United Arab Emirates Political Overview

The President of the UAE is the Ruler of Abu Dhabi, Sheikh Khalifa bin Zayed al-Nahyan. He has the full backing of the ruling families in the other six Emirates. The Vice President and Prime Minister is the Ruler of Dubai, Sheikh Mohammed bin Rashid al-Maktoum. His priority is Dubai's business development but he still takes a keen interest in regional politics. Both President and Vice President have appointed Crown Princes to ensure a smooth line of succession.

The Federation is governed by the Supreme Council comprised of the Rulers of the seven Emirates. The Council is advised by the 40 strong Federal National Council (FNC), with 20 members elected by the 6,689 handpicked members of the Electoral College and the other 20 nominated by their respective Emirates.

The UAE foreign policy remains a balance between the maintenance of its strategic alliances with the west and the imperative of maintaining friendly relations with Iran, with whom the UAE enjoys strong historical trade relations.

Abu Dhabi, Dubai & the Northern Emirates

Abu Dhabi is the capital of the UAE and has approximately 10% of the world's proven oil reserves and 5% of the gas. The Emirate also has an impressive investment portfolio financed from oil income. And has traditionally been the cornerstone of the economy with large proven reserves. Abu Dhabi is diversifying its activities with the development of new industrial cities, real estate developments and other major projects including ports, airport expansion and new hotels.

Dubai's economy developed at a huge rate from 2000-8 and has established itself as the regions exhibition, financial, trade and tourism hub. It has a significant infrastructure base and is service accessible, with over 170 shipping lines and about 100 airlines.

The Northern Emirates of Sharjah, Fujairah, Ajman, Umm Al Quwain and Ras Al Khaimah each have their own commercial profile and economic priorities. Each Emirate has a port, most of which are running at near capacity and have expansion programmes to cope with increasing demand. Major industries for the smaller emirates include agriculture, tourism and nice manufacturing ventures.

Sharjah is the third largest of the emirates and home to two-thirds of the UAE's manufacturing base. It has a fast growing international airport, two free zones and two active ports. The emirate is more conservative than Dubai; alcohol is illegal and Sharjah's decency law requires that people dress more conservatively than in Dubai.

Ajman is situated to the Northwest of Sharjah and home to a variety of factories producing goods including foodstuffs, beverages, tobacco, textiles, leather goods, paper products and readymade garments. Ajman also has a thriving boat building industry, manufacturing boats ranging from traditional wooden to more sophisticated luxury yachts.

Fujairah is situated on the Gulf of Oman. The Fujairah port was deepened and extended in 1985 in order to attract new shipping lines and new business. The port gives access to the UAE without the need to enter the Gulf through the Straits of Hormuz and is among the top three bunkering ports in the world. A number of ongoing projects include power generation, water desalination and hotel construction.

Umm Al Quwain has a variety of industrial developments with a cement factory, manufacturing units producing pipes and corrugated sheets. Agriculture is an important part of the local economy and a number of different crops are grown. The emirate is also home to a large poultry farm.

Ras Al Khaimah (RAK) is north east of Umm Al Quwain and is the main farming area of the Northern Emirates. Mining is also one of the foremost activities; there are two quarries and four cement plants. There are also factories producing tiles and ceramics, glass tableware and pharmaceuticals. Some oil exploration is underway. With a deepwater port situated near the Straits of hormuz, RAK is in a good location. The emirate has established a free zone and is also developing a $1 billion resort and hi-tech part, Jazirat Al Hamrah, combining luxury waterfront residential and resort apartments with a technology park. There is also considerable agricultural potential with 15% of land under cultivation. Several large companies are also involved in dairy products, livestock and poultry production.

Chapter 4: Characteristics of United Arab Emirates Market

To do business in the UAE, it is necessary to comply with the federal laws governing business activity. It is essential to obtain the correct authorisation and licences prior to conducting trade within the UAE. In addition it is important to be properly advised as to the requirements which apply in each particular Emirate.

In the private sector, there is nothing to prevent a foreign principal from supplying its customers directly in the UAE. If the foreign principal therefore already has an established customer base in the country it may not be necessary to appoint an agent. If however the foreign principal's potential business is substantial or no established client base exists, it may be appropriate to appoint an agent.

As far as the public sector is concerned, most governmental ministries and public sector organisations will only deal through an agent. If an agent is to be appointed then the foreign principal must comply with the various requirements laid down by law. Perhaps the most fundamental requirement is that only UAE citizens, or companies which are wholly owned by UAE citizens, are permitted to conduct the business of an agent.

It is therefore not possible for foreign nationals or a company incorporated in the UAE which has any foreign participation to conduct these activities. For the avoidance of doubt, other GCC nationals or companies incorporated in other GCC states cannot act as agents in the UAE either alone or in partnership with a UAE national or company.

Foriegn companies wishing to approach the UAE market are advised to undertake market research and plan market entry.

Chapter 5: Exporting to United Arab Emirates

Economic activity in the UAE is regulated by each individual Emirate as well as by the Federal Government. Dubai has taken the lead in constructing/developing a relatively unrestricted environment in which to do business. Competition is very keen in established sectors. Breaking into an existing market means newcomers have to work hard to capture a share. Newcomers need to find competitive advantages, for example, better quality, faster delivery, lower prices or newer designs.

Other opportunities exist alongside notable joint public / private stock companies. An example is Dubai Investments, a Public Joint Stock Company, which is developing a 3180 hectare industrial park on the outskirts of Dubai. The company has interests in the manufacturing of consumer goods, communications, light industry, high technology and environmentally friendly acquisitions. Their core business is investment in viable projects that have the potential for growth across all economic sectors.

Selling in the UAE

The majority of local governments and federal ministries based in Dubai are required to purchase through local agents, who may also assist in marketing and sales, although it is still possible for a company outside the UAE to sell directly to contractors.

Generally, price is the most important factor in promoting sales, although it is evident that product quality and after-sales service are also important selling factors in the UAE market. Advertising and participation in sales promotions and trade exhibitions is often helpful for raising consumer awareness and gaining market share, but effectiveness will vary according to product.

The period from September-June sees a variety of trade exhibitions and conferences in a broad range of sectors including information technology, education, interior design, construction and health. Exhibitions and trade fairs are also held in Sharjah, Ras Al Khaimah and Fujairah.

Channels of Distribution and Sale

There are three main methods of exporting to Dubai and the Northern Emirates. It is up to individual companies to choose the method of export that best suits the characteristics of their product or service following careful assessment of potential sales in the market place. These methods are:

Direct Trade

International manufacturers and exporters may conduct business with the country by concluding transactions directly with importers and traders who are already established in the market. This type of trade is best suited to low volume trade or to test the market and should not otherwise be used as a permanent arrangement.

Commercial Agencies

A foreign company wishing to supply goods to Dubai and the Northern Emirates can do so without establishing a physical presence by appointing a commercial agent and distributor. The Federal Commercial Agency Laws of 1981 and 1988 state that an agent must be a UAE national or a company 100% owned by UAE nationals. There have been suggestions that this law may be reviewed. Officials from the UAE have met with a delegation from the World Trade Organisation (WTO), as part of the drafting process for a new UAE commercial law currently under consideration. The UAE, which has been a member of the WTO since 1996, held discussions with the organisation ahead of a trade policy review scheduled for March 2006, the date when the ten year exemptions from some WTO regulations that the country secured on joining the organisation expire. The new law though still to be agreed will allow majority foreign ownership of UAE registered firms; at present foreigners can only own 100% of UAE companies in dedicated free zones such at Jebel Ali and Dubai Internet City.

The UAE is a federal country and it may be necessary to appoint more than one representative in order to cover the whole market effectively. Alternatively a sole agent may be appointed. In practice, many overseas companies appoint several agents to cover defined areas of the country (and the region) and may have separate agreements for separate products. Any commercial agency agreement needs to be drawn up with great care specifying the products and territories to be covered by the agent.

The Commercial Agencies Law was amended in 2006. Under the new law the provision prohibiting a principle from refusing to renew an agency agreement without justified cause has been deleted. In reality it may still be extremely difficult to terminate a commercial agency agreement without facing a claim for compensation from the agent unless it is terminated with the written agreement of both parties. However, Article 8 also now states that a principle may register a different agent if the term of the agreement has expired. Under the New Law that either the principle or the agent may claim compensation if termination of the agency causes damage to either of the parties.

We recommend that foreign companies should seek legal advice before entering into a written agreement.

Chapter 6: Setting Up a Presence in Dubai

Apart from the obvious distinct advantages of having a physical presence in the market place, one important consideration is that businessmen in the Middle East prefer to meet, in person, those they may wish to do business with. It is important to invest time in building relationships with potential customers or partners.

Under federal legislation, the principal relevant options available for conducting business in the UAE are:

1. Participation in a local company or other commercial entity.
2. Establishment of a branch office.
3. Establishment of a branch or subsidiary in one of the Free Zones of the UAE.
4. Appointment of a commercial agent or distributor.

Which of the above options is the most appropriate will usually depend upon the nature of the activities proposed to be undertaken and it may be that a combination of the options outlined is appropriate for your particular business.

Establishment of a local company or other commercial entity

There is no such thing as an "off the shelf" company in the UAE. Every commercial entity must be specifically established. This is neither a simple nor a speedy process. The most common commercial entity used by foreign companies is the LLC. Legal support is advisable as to all aspects of establishing a UAE company or other commercial entity including, for example, its capitalisation and level of foreign participation. Foreign participation is generally limited to no more than 49% (although there are contractual ways in which to mitigate the effects of a minority ownership of shares) and general partners in any of the partnerships listed above must be UAE nationals.

Establishment of a branch office

The scope of activities permitted to be undertaken by branch offices varies from Emirate to Emirate, although generally a broad range of commercial trading activities can be undertaken. A foreign company establishing a branch office in one of the Emirates must obtain consent from the Ministry of Economy before a local business licence from the government of the relevant Emirate is issued. Furthermore, the applicant company is now required to deposit a bank guarantee in the sum of AED 50,000 to the Ministry of Economy. The branch office must also be sponsored by a UAE national or by a locally registered company wholly owned by UAE nationals. The sponsor is known as the National Agent. A formal National Agency Agreement is required, in which the National Agent undertakes to sponsor and assist the foreign company, usually in return for a fee. It is not advisable for a National Agency Agreement to be signed without legal advice having been taken. In certain businesses, the permission of a particular authority is required, for example the Municipality in Dubai as regards engineering consultancy and the Central Bank as regards finance.

Using the Free Zones of the UAE

The UAE has free zones in most of the individual Emirates. Dubai also has a number of specialist free zones, including Jebel Ali Free Zone, Dubai Airport Free Zone, Dubai Multi Commodities Centre, Dubai Internet City, Dubai Media City and Dubai Healthcare City. A media free zone was launched in Abu Dhabi in October 2008.

The free zones, offer a variety of valuable benefits to businesses and a degree of flexibility, includes:
1. 100% foreign ownership through branches, single or multiple shareholder companies (known as FZEs,FZCOs or FZ-LLCs).
2. No National Agent required for branch offices of foreign companies.
3. No customs duties on imports and re-exports (except re-exports into onshore UAE).
4. Special assistance in obtaining work permits for staff.
5. Guaranteed exemptions from corporate taxes.

Details of the incentives and facilities available, together with registration, minimum capitalisation and other requirements vary between free zones, and specific advice should be taken.

Chapter 7: Customs Duties and Regulations

Customs Duties

The UAE imposes 5% customs duty across-the-board on most categories of imports. Products brought into a free zone within the UAE are exempt from import duties. The UAE's customs tariffs are based on the Customs Co-operation Council's nomenclature system. Duties may be levied ad valorem or specific to the goods concerned.

Foodstuff, medicines and goods destined for government or oil companies are generally exempt from duty. Customs duties are levied on the CIF value at the rate of five per cent. Where permitted, the duty on alcoholic beverages is 50 per cent and on tobacco products is 100 per cent.

Sharjah, Ras Al Khaimah, Ajman, Fujairah and Umm Al Quwain customs duties are levied on the CIF value. In Sharjah, there are two free zones at Hamriya and the airport. Free zones are also operated in Ajman, Fujairah, Ras Al Khaimah and Umm Al Quwain (see section 4 for contact details).

Additional Taxes

1. **Corporate income tax:** the individual emirates issue corporate tax decrees although in practice, taxes have only been imposed on

oil and gas producing companies and petrochemical producing companies at rates set out in their government concession agreements.

2. **Capital gains tax:** capital gains are not subject to taxation.
3. **Social security taxes:** the UAE does not impose social security taxes.

Commercial law

The Federal Commercial Code has been in effect since 1993 and is a wide ranging law, which directly affects every commercial organisation conducting business in the UAE. The Commercial Code covers such matters as the regulation of commercial activities, including preparation of commercial contracts, and obligations and assumptions that will apply in the absence of express agreement to the contrary.

Enforcement of your commercial rights

The UAE has civil courts, which deal specifically with civil and commercial matters and are governed by strict rules of procedure. The courts of Dubai do not form part of the federal court system but do apply the federal Civil Procedures Code. Although contracts prepared in languages other than Arabic are enforceable before the courts, all pleadings and supporting documentation must be prepared in or translated into Arabic. There is a right of appeal against judgments in given circumstances.

Specific advice should be taken on the potential length and cost of any action prior to commencing proceedings in the UAE. In addition, arbitration should be considered as an alternative means of dispute resolution. The Chambers of Commerce and Industry in both Abu Dhabi and Dubai have established commercial arbitration centres. The UAE has now acceded to the 1958 New York Convention on the Recognition and Enforcement of Foreign Arbitral Awards. This means that foreign arbitral awards should be more easily enforceable in the UAE.

Government contracts

Companies doing business with official bodies should note that there are strict regulations affecting government contracts. Also, government bodies operate various standard forms of contract, such as construction and consultancy contracts, which follow international practice but are adapted for local usage. Standard forms of contract also vary between the different Emirates.

Real estate

Although the UAE Civil Code includes a number of provisions dealing with land ownership, leasing, co ownership of floors and apartments and the creation and operation of owners' associations, it does not address the underlying issue of the ownership of property by non-UAE nationals. It has therefore been left to each of the individual Emirates to legislate on real estate matters. The Dubai property law (Law No.

7 of 2006) provides the general rule that property ownership in the Emirate shall be restricted to UAE and GCC nationals (and companies wholly owned by them), as well as public shareholding companies, and that other nationalities may be granted a right of property ownership on a freehold or 99 year leasehold basis, in 30 pre-designated areas. In 2007 laws were introduced requiring developers to establish escrow accounts designed to protect off plan purchasers, and concerning the multiple ownership of property.

Traditionally in Abu Dhabi, absolute ownership of land has been vested in the government of Abu Dhabi, which has tended only to grant rights in land to Abu Dhabi nationals and companies 100% owned by UAE nationals. However, Abu Dhabi Law No. 19 of 2005 and Law No. 2 of 2007 altered this position and made available a wider range of property rights to UAE nationals, GCC nationals and expatriates. GCC nationals have the right to own land and buildings in Abu Dhabi, and other expatriates the right to own buildings in certain designated "investment areas". Federally non-UAE and GCC nationals may also acquire a right of usufruct (effectively a lease) for up to 99 years, or a right of musataha (the right to develop the land of another) for up to 50 years, each renewable by mutual consent.

Generally, despite the introduction of a number of significant laws which have been passed in order to regulate property ownership and property related transactions in the UAE, there are still important issues which arise from the ownership of land, for example in relation to inheritance and rights of residence.

Debt Collection

In order to minimise the risk of accruing bad debts; exporters should take up credit references on UAE importers with whom they do business. Legal action can be both costly and lengthy and may not be worthwhile for relatively small debts.

Taxation

Certain Emirates, including Abu Dhabi and Dubai, have promulgated income tax legislation but, in practice, it is only applied to companies in the oil, gas and related sectors, and branches of foreign banks. Customs duties are currently levied at a general rate of 5% within the GCC, in accordance with the GCC Customs Union. There is no direct personal taxation in the UAE. Most Emirates levy various municipal taxes and indirect taxation through official fees is commonplace

Importing Goods

Goods which have been manufactured in Israel may not be imported into the UAE. Pornographic material, ivory/rhino horns, cannabis, alcoholic beverages, fire-arms, fireworks, narcotics and opium are also strictly prohibited. British and Irish beef and related products may not be imported. All printed matter, films and tapes must be cleared by the Ministry of Information. Exports to the UAE are subject to pre-shipment inspection for those who want it.

Responding to Tenders

Foreign tenderers for military (and some civil) supply and service contracts are required to pre-qualify, under the UAE Offset Programme, which includes signing an Offset Agreement with the UAE Offsets Group (UOG). The Offset Agreement will require a successful tenderer to earn credits by promoting economic activity in the UAE, through direct investment in projects and otherwise. It is strongly recommended that companies required to sign an Offset Agreement take appropriate legal and other professional advice on its implications.

Employment legislation

There are legislative and other requirements governing the employment of Emirati and expatriate labour in the UAE. These impose certain rights and obligations on both the employer and the employee. To some extent, these differ as between expatriate employees who are brought into the country by their employer and those who are employed locally.

Immigration

Sponsorship by a company of expatriate personnel and visitors to the UAE imposes obligations on that company, and its authorised representatives or managers, as to the conduct of such persons. There are various regulations concerning the issue, renewal and cancellation of visas and labour cards. Great care must be taken not to infringe such regulations and UAE-based employees must respect the customs and laws of the UAE.

Documentation

The necessary documents required for import and export of goods to and from the UAE are as follows;
1. Invoices – initiated by supplier
2. Certificate of Origin
3. Bills of Lading / Airway Bill

Labelling and Packaging Regulations

Labelling in Arabic is required on all consumer products. Labels need to provide information including details of the manufacturer, product information, and standard quality disclosures. There are some products which must be clearly marked, stamped, branded or labelled so as to indicate the country of origin. Additionally, many food products may also have to comply with hygiene and ingredients regulations. Labels on foodstuffs must have the following information:
1. Product and brand names.
2. Production and expiration dates.
3. Country of origin.
4. Name of the manufacturer.
5. A comprehensive list of ingredients and additives.

All the emirates have modern ports and warehouse facilities. The port of Jebel Ali in Dubai is the largest man-made port in the world; it currently has 63 deepwater berths and good warehousing facilities. An expansion of the port is underway. The majority of goods are imported by sea. Much is transferred by truck to neighbouring GCC countries or to smaller ships for onward movement to ports around the region.

In Dubai, Port Rashid and Jebel Ali Port are now amalgamated under the Dubai Ports World. Port Rashid is one of the busiest ports in the Gulf and has 35 berths.

The development of the free zones at Jebel Ali and Dubai International Airport has enabled Dubai to dominate the regional business of unloading, breaking down, and reloading cargo for onward shipment. Warehouse facilities provide storage for imports and there are no storage charges for the first 20 days.

Delivery Dates

Sea freight from the UK takes approximately 4-6 weeks, with airfreight taking 3-7 days. Goods requiring transfer from the ports will require extra time and this will need to be taken into account when calculating delivery time. Customs clearance can also add a week or two to delivery times.

The British International Freight Association's (BIFA) importer/exporter initiative aims to provide specialist help and assistance to companies who are new to exporting. This service, available through selected BIFA registered members, offers up to one day's free consultancy to advice companies on such matters as modes of transport, distribution methods, costing, documentation and payment terms.

Anti Dumping and Countervailing

As a signatory to the World Trade Organisation (WTO), the UAE can apply anti-dumping or countervailing duties to products which are sold in the UAE for less than they sell in the country of origin in order to gain market share or undermine an existing or emerging industry in the UAE. These additional duties are imposed on a temporary basis to counteract the effects of an unfairly low price or an unfair subsidy to the producer. An example of an unfair subsidy would be government grants, capital loans, favourable loan guarantees, export rebates, or tax incentives. These duties can only be imposed if the imported goods have caused, or are likely to cause, material harm to the UAE domestic market.

Chapter 8: Business Etiquette, Language and Culture

The UAE has a diverse and multi-cultural society taking into consideration that 80% of the UAE population are expatriates. This has meant that the UAE is regarded as relatively liberal within the region and provides schools, cultural centres and restaurants that cater for international cultures. The national culture mainly revolves around the religion of Islam, although other religions are also respected whereby churches and temples can be found alongside mosques.

The Islamic dress code is not compulsory, unlike in neighbouring Saudi Arabia. Most UAE national (Emiratis) males prefer to wear a kandura, an ankle-length white shirt and most Emirati women wear an abaya, a black over garment covering most part of the body. This attire is particularly well suited for the UAE's hot and dry climate. Western style clothing is, however, dominant due to the large expatriate population and this practice is beginning to grow in popularity among Emiratis.

Language

English is widely spoken throughout the country and where possible translators are available. Whilst it is preferable for written correspondence to be English, Arabic is sometimes preferred within some public sector organisations.

Meetings and Presentations

As in other countries, more than anything it is important to target the right person in your contacts, the decision-maker. It is also preferable to establish new business contacts via an introduction by mutual contact, exhibitions, networking receptions.

Face-to-face meetings are preferred as phone or emails are sometimes seen as impersonal. Appointments should be made no more than 2 weeks in advance and confirmed a few days before the actual meeting as priorities may change.

The working week within the private sector is Sunday-Thursday from 9am-5pm and within the public sector Saturday-Wednesday from 8am-2.30pm (some offices are open until 4pm).

There are many exhibitions that take place in the UAE with some of the largest regional events held in Dubai and Abu Dhabi. This is a good opportunity for companies to meet potential partners, distributors and clients.

Negotiations

Personal contact with potential and existing partners/clients and regular visits to the market are of the utmost importance and it is natural for the business relationship to be built with time. It is advised that you consult a lawyer prior to signing an agreement in the UAE.

Chapter 9: Challenges of Doing Business in United Arab Emirates

The UAE does not present major challenges to UK companies wishing to develop trade. However, there may be some specific issues which British companies should consider, namely as far as language and terms of payment are concerned.

Getting Paid - Terms of Payment

Most UK banks can provide advice on payment. Generally speaking any of the customary methods of payment used in international commercial transactions can be used when doing business with UAE companies. Irrevocable Letter of Credits (L/C) and cash against documents (CAD) terms are the most common methods of payment.

How to Invest in the UAE

The UK is the largest investor in Dubai with US$4.2 billion, followed by Japan, India, USA and the Netherlands. The Dubai Statistics Centre revealed that the volume of foreign direct investment (FDI) in Dubai increased to US$11.6 billion in 2006, showing an increase of 13.4% of the previous year.

The UAE Commercial Companies Law, Federal Law No 8 of 1984 (as amended by Federal Law No 13 of

1988), governs the activities of foreign companies in the UAE.

Investment Promotion and Protection Agreements (IPPAs) are designed to encourage investor confidence by setting high standards of investor protection applicable in international law.

Key elements include provisions for equal and non-discriminatory treatment of investors and their investments, compensation for expropriation, transfer of capital and returns and access to independent settlement of disputes.

In 2009, the UAE was ranked 30 out of 180 countries, (ranked 35 in 2008) in Transparency International's corruption perception index (CPI).

Terrorism Threat

The geographical location of the UAE in the Persian Gulf and Arabian Peninsula region, and the threat of al-Qaida (or other allied groups) looking to target Western interests in the Gulf (specifically in the UAE) both serve to raise the threat. Al-Qaida continues to release statements calling for the removal of western interests from the Gulf, and we judge that the UAE is viewed as a viable target for an attack. The association with Western commercial interests, the use of the UAE as a regional transit hub between east and west, and the large expatriate population all contribute to the potential threat.

Chapter 10: Intellectual Property

IP rights are territorial, that is they only give protection in the countries where they are granted or registered. If you are thinking about trading internationally, you should consider registering your IP rights in your export markets.

Federal intellectual property (IP) laws have been in place in the United Arab Emirates since 1992 for the protection and enforcement of intellectual property rights. Further, in 2002, a major legislative overhaul resulted in amending/repealing 1992 laws to meet international standards for intellectual property protection.

The United Arab Emirates is a party to the following main intellectual property protection Treaties:
1. The Paris Convention for the Protection of Industrial Property covering patents and trademarks.
2. Berne Convention (for Literary and Artistic Works).
3. Patent Cooperation Treaty (PCT).
4. Rome Convention (for Performers, Producers of Phonograms and Broadcasting Organizations).
5. WIPO Copyright Treaty (WCT).
6. WIPO Performances and Phonograms Treaty (WPPT).
7. The Agreement on Trade-Related Aspects of Intellectual Property Rights (TRIPS Agreement), which forms one of the main

Agreements of the World Trade Organization (WTO).

Below are brief highlights of the basic elements of the intellectual property laws of the United Arab Emirates:

Trademarks

Applicable Legislation: Federal Law No. 37 for the year 1992 (as amended by the Federal Law No. 8 for the year 2002).

Duration of the Right: A trademark registration is valid for 10 years as of the date of filing the application renewable for similar periods.

Sanctions against Infringement: A trademark can be infringed by manufacturing, sale and possession of counterfeit goods, as well as imitation, misleading practices, and fraudulent use of registered trademarks. Minimum fines of GBP 935 can be levied and/or prison sentences can be imposed on the infringers. The court has authority to order seizure, confiscation and destruction infringing goods and the equipment/machinery used to commit infringement. The court further has authority to publish the judgment in local Newspapers or the Federal Gazette.

Copyrights

Applicable Legislation: Federal Law No. 7 for the year 2002.

Duration of the Right: The duration of protection is for the lifetime of the author plus 50 years after his death or 50 years from the date of publication in cases of cinematographic works, works of corporate bodies and works published for the first time after the death of the author.

Sanctions against Infringement: Copyrights infringement attracts a jail term and/or a fine of not less than GBP 1,870. The court has authority to order seizure, confiscation and destruction infringing goods and the equipment/machinery used to commit infringement. The court further has authority to publish the judgment in local Newspapers or the Federal Gazette.

Patents

Applicable Legislation: Federal Law No. 17 for the year 2002.

Duration of the Right: A patent is valid for 20 years only with annuities payable during that time.

Sanctions against Infringement: The penalties stated in the Law for violators of patent rights are fines of not less than GBP 935 and/or imprisonment. The court has authority to order confiscation and destruction of the seizures, tools, or machines and removal of the violating material. The court further has authority to publish the judgment in local Newspapers or the Federal Gazette.

Designs

Applicable Legislation: Federal Law No. 17 for the year 2002.

Duration of the Right: Registration of a Design is valid for 10 years only with annuities payable during that time.

Sanctions against Infringement: The infringement of design right attracts the punishment of a fine of not less than GBP 935 and/or imprisonment. The court has authority to order confiscation and destruction of the seizures, tools, or machines and removal of the violating material. The court further has authority to publish the judgement in local Newspapers or the Federal Gazette.

Chapter 11: Construction Opportunities in the United Arab Emirates

The UAE ranks among the top countries in the region in terms of business environment and relative openness. It is recognised as a leading trading hub and a launch pad for companies looking to do business in the MENA region. The country is also considered a safe haven in the Middle East. The UAE economy is increasingly becoming diversified, gradually shifting focus away from oil and gas. The diversification strategy has paved the way for large construction, infrastructure development and cultural projects offering a myriad of opportunities across sectors such as.

Saadiyat Island development is a mixed use commercial, residential and leisure project currently underway. The main attraction of the project is the cultural district which will be home to four museums – Zayed National Museum, Louvre Abu Dhabi, Guggenheim Abu Dhabi and a maritime museum. The individual museum projects are in various stages and the development is being overseen by the Tourism Development and Investment Company. These projects are expected to be completed over the next 3 to 6 years.

Habtoor Palace is a USD 1.3 billion hotel and theatre project recently announced by the Al Habtoor Group. Habtoor Palace will include hotels, theatre, banqueting and meetings facilities and a shopping arcade. Earlier last year French broadcaster Fashion TV announced an agreement with Habtoor Group to build a five star Fashion Hotel.

Establishment of a Cultural District in Dubai was announced recently. The district will include a Modern Art Museum and an opera house. Further details are awaited

Chapter 12: Financial Services Opportunities in the United Arab Emirates

Within the UAE, financial services activity is focused in Dubai; Dubai has the largest and most sophisticated financial services industry in the region being home to many banks, insurance, financial and legal services firms. Abu Dhabi and Dubai are growth markets in their own right in many areas of interest to UK financial services industry from which many UK firms have already set up shop accessing a significantly growing regional market.

In the UAE there are effectively two financial services markets 1st Dubai International Financial Centre (DIFC), regulated by Dubai Financial Services Authority (DFSA), a hub for institutional finance and a gateway for capital and investment to GCC and MENA region and 2nd the federally regulated market.

The DIFC is emerging as a key regulatory environment, using mainly English common law and arbitration, with asset management and insurance being some key activities. In addition, being close to some of the largest and most active and diversified sovereign wealth funds not only help cement relationships, but also facilitates inward investment into the UK.

The Abu Dhabi government owns one of the world's biggest investment funds, ADIA, which has estimated reserves of between US$500-900 billion.

Private Public Partnerships (PPP)

The global economic slowdown, limited liquidity and relative scarcity of credit have led many regional governments to consider PPP as a serious means of financing public sector projects. A recently published statement by an official from Dubai's Roads and Transport Authority (RTA) stated that it will seek private funding for almost a third of its infrastructure projects over the next five years. The Dubai PPP law according to senior officials is being finalised.

The priority for Dubai Government up to year 2012 is delivery of mass transport projects handled by the RTA followed by Power and Water (as longer term issues) delivered by Dubai Electricity and Water Authority (DEWA). Also, the ambitious levels of growth in Abu Dhabi 2030 strategy require more private and public partnership to ensure delivery of its objectives though leaning towards services delivery with some private participation and funding.

The identified opportunities shadowed in sectors like mass transport and energy such as the Etihad Railways project valued at £11 Billion, Al Sufouh project valued at £600 Million and Dubai's Independent Power Plant (IPP) project valued at £1.35 Billion.

Chapter 13: Conclusion

Bouncing cheques and unpaid bills can mean prison

As Hastie's Appleby found, "fraudulent practices", which include dishonoured cheques and unpaid bills, can result in imprisonment or fines. Those attempting to leave the UAE with unpaid debts may be detained.

Don't ask after the health of female relatives

You should attempt to chat with business associates to establish a trusting relationship, and asking about your associate's well-being is fine. However, the well-being of a businessman's wife or female relatives is regarded as a private matter, and enquiries along these lines may offend. Similarly, do not include an associate's wife in an invitation to dine with you, unless you have prior indication that she is likely to accept.

Don't get caught with drugs

The UAE has a zero tolerance policy towards illegal drugs. Penalties can include the death sentence or life imprisonment, and some medications available over the counter or by prescription in Western World are illegal in the UAE. The presence of illegal drugs detected in blood or urine tests is considered possession, and you can be charged with possessing drugs if trace amounts are found on your body, clothing or luggage. Amounts of 0.05 grams or less can lead to guilty verdicts.

It is illegal for your employer to hold onto your passport

Foreign employees may be asked to leave their passports with employers as a condition of employment in the UAE. While this practice is not unusual, it is against the law. Westerners intending to work in the UAE should clearly establish the terms and conditions of their employment or sponsorship at the beginning of their employment to minimise the risk of contractual or labour disputes. Should a dispute arise, the UAE Ministry of Labour has established a special department to review and arbitrate labour claims.

You need a permit to drink

Drinking or possession of alcohol for UAE residents without a UAE Ministry of Interior liquor permit is illegal and can lead to arrest and imprisonment. Alcohol is served in some hotels and sold in a limited number of designated stores, and it may only be purchased from stores by people who hold a liquor licence. These licences are only available to UAE residents and only permit the holder to purchase or consume alcohol in the emirate which issued the licence.

Alcohol consumption and pork are completely illegal in the Emirate of Sharjah.

During the holy month of Ramadan, eating, drinking and smoking between sunrise and sunset is forbidden for Muslims. Non-Muslims are also expected to refrain from eating, drinking and smoking in public in front of Muslims between sunrise and sunset. A small number of large establishments, such as five star hotels, will cater for non-Muslims

Dress modestly

Standard business dress for men is a business suit and tie. Evening functions can require anything from a sports coat to a business suit with tie and, on casual occasions, trousers and a shirt are acceptable.

Women should wear loose fitting clothing and dress conservatively, avoiding short skirts or revealing blouses, but their heads need not be covered.

Do not admire your host's possessions

It is common to exchange gifts in business circles, but items are usually limited to small corporate items such as pens and brochures. Guests should take care not to express admiration for something owned by their host, as they may have the object offered to them immediately, according to an ancient custom still observed in many traditional areas.

Address Gulf nationals by their first names

Gulf nationals are usually addressed by their first name. For example, a Mr Khalid bin Abdallah Al Thani's first name is Khalid, he is the son of Abdallah, and his family group or tribe is Al Thani. He would therefore be called Mr Khalid.

Business is often conducted with non-Arab managers, many of whom will likely be of Indian origin. Many Indians do not use surnames, and often the initial of their father's name is placed in front of their own name. An A. Sivam would be referred to as Mr Sivam, with the A representing the father's name. Indian women generally take their husband's name on marriage, so a Miss R. Selvarajan could become Mrs A. Sivam or Mrs Sivam Selvarajan.

Drink that coffee

At business meetings, coffee or tea is generally offered to guests in order of their rank. Guests should always accept initial offerings and may accept more than one cup, but never any more than the host or others present. You can signify that you've had sufficient coffee by shaking your cup when handing it back to the server.

It's a tax haven

Unless you're a bank or an oil company, you are not required to pay income or consumption tax in the United Arab Emirates. Foreign banks pay a 20% tax on their profits and foreign oil companies pay taxes and royalties on their proceeds. Imports generally incur a 5% customs duty, with the exception of some luxury goods such as tobacco, which is levied at 50-70%.

Good Luck!

Part 2: CEO Guide to Doing Business in Saudi Arabia

Chapter 14: Introduction

Saudi Arabia's command economy is petroleum-based; roughly 75% of budget revenues and 90% of export earnings come from the oil industry. The oil industry comprises about 45% of Saudi Arabia's gross domestic product, compared with 40% from the private sector. Saudi Arabia officially has about 260 billion barrels (4.1×1010 m3) of oil reserves, comprising about one-fifth of the world's proven total petroleum reserves.

The government is attempting to promote growth in the private sector by privatizing industries such as power and telecommunications. Saudi Arabia announced plans to begin privatizing the electricity companies in 1999, which followed the ongoing privatization of the telecommunications company. Shortages of water and rapid population growth may constrain government efforts to increase self-sufficiency in agricultural products.

In the 1990s, Saudi Arabia experienced a significant contraction of oil revenues combined with a high rate of population growth. Per capita income fell from a high of $11,700 at the height of the oil boom in 1981 to $6,300 in 1998. Increases in oil prices since 2000 have helped boost per capita GDP to $17,000 in 2007 dollars, or about $7,400 adjusted for inflation.

Oil price increases of 2008–2009 have triggered a second oil boom, pushing Saudi Arabia's budget surplus to $28 billion (110SR billion) in 2005.

Tadawul (the Saudi stock market index) finished 2004 with a massive 76.23% to close at 4437.58 points. Market capitalization was up 110.14% from a year earlier to stand at $157.3 billion (589.93SR billion), which makes it the biggest stock market in the Middle East.

OPEC (the Organization of Petroleum Exporting Countries) limits its members' oil production based on their "proven reserves." The higher their reserves, the more OPEC allows them to produce. Saudi Arabia's published reserves have shown little change since 1980, with the main exception being an increase of about 100 billion barrels (1.6×1010 m3) between 1987 and 1988.

Saudi Arabia is one of only a few fast-growing countries in the world with a relatively high per capita income of $24,200 (2010). Saudi Arabia will be launching six "economic cities" (e.g. King Abdullah Economic City) which are planned to be completed by 2020. These six new industrialized cities are intended to diversify the economy of Saudi Arabia, and are expected to increase the per capita income. The King of Saudi Arabia has announced that the per capita income is forecast to rise from $15,000 in 2006 to $33,500 in 2020. The cities will be spread around Saudi Arabia to promote diversification for each region and their economy, and the cities are projected to contribute $150 billion to the GDP.

However the urban areas of Riyadh and Jeddah are expected to contribute $287 billion dollars by the year 2020.

Chapter 15: Political Process and Opposition in Saudi Arabia

In the absence of national elections and political parties, politics in Saudi Arabia takes place in two distinct arenas: within the royal family, the Al Saud, and between the royal family and the rest of Saudi society. The royal family is politically divided by factions based on clan loyalties, personal ambitions and ideological differences. The most powerful clan faction is known as the 'Sudairi Seven', comprising the late King Fahd and his full brothers and their descendants. Ideological divisions include issues over the speed and direction of reform, and whether the role of the ulema should be increased or reduced.

There were divisions within the family over who should succeed to the throne after the accession or earlier death of Prince Sultan. When Prince Sultan died before ascending to the throne on October 21, 2011, King Abdullah appointed Prince Nayef as crown prince. Price Nayef also died before ascending to the throne in 2012.

Outside of the Al-Saud, participation in the political process is limited to a relatively small segment of the population and takes the form of the royal family consulting with the ulema, tribal sheikhs and members of important commercial families on major decisions. This process is not reported by the Saudi media. In theory, all males of full age have a right to petition the king directly through the traditional tribal meeting known as the majlis. In many ways the approach to government differs little from the traditional system of tribal rule. Tribal identity remains strong and, outside of the royal family, political influence is frequently determined by tribal affiliation, with tribal sheikhs maintaining a considerable degree of influence over local and national events. As mentioned earlier, in recent years there have been limited steps to widen political participation such as the establishment of the Consultative Council in the early 1990s and the National Dialogue Forum in 2003.

The rule of the Al Saud faces political opposition from four sources: Sunni Islamist activism; liberal critics; the underground Green Party of Saudi Arabia; the Shi'ite minority particularly in the Eastern Province; and long-standing tribal and regional particularistic opponents (for example in the Hejaz). Of these, the Islamic activists have been the most prominent threat to the regime and have in recent years perpetrated a number of violent or terrorist acts in the country. However, open protest against the government, even if peaceful, is not tolerated. On 29 January 2011, hundreds of protesters gathered in the city of Jeddah in a rare display of criticism against the city's poor infrastructure after deadly floods swept through the city, killing eleven people. Police stopped the demonstration after about 15 minutes and arrested 30 to 50 people. As part of the wave of protests and revolutions affecting the Middle East and North Africa in early 2011, a number of incidents and protests occurred in Saudi Arabia

Chapter 16: Opportunities in Saudi Arabia

Saudi Arabia's fast-growing economy is creating opportunities for both exporters and investors. These are further boosted by moves to diversify the economy away from dependence on oil and gas, economic reform, market liberalisation and a growing private sector. There are opportunities at all levels in.

1. **Infrastructure:** There are new and upgrade projects across all sectors including industrial and economic cities, prisons, ports and airports.
2. **Major sporting or other events:** It will be a few years before Saudi Arabia hosts major sporting events; however, there are plans to build a major sports city.
3. **Resilience and Disaster recovery:** Saudi Arabia hosts hundreds of thousands of visitors who perform Hajj every year. Major floods in Jeddah have highlighted the need for planning and recovery.
4. **Maritime Security:** Major new ports planned, including Jizan and King Abdullah Economic Cities.
5. **Border Control:** There are several projects under Border control, for example physical barriers.

Saudi Arabia is the UK's largest trading partner in the Middle East with UK's export of goods amounting to £2.19 billion in 2008. Saudi Arabia's fast-growing economy is creating opportunities which are further boosted by moves to diversify the economy away from dependence on oil and gas, economic reform, market liberalisation and a growing private sector.

Local representation

Saudi Law does not require foreign companies to appoint a commercial agent to do business in the Kingdom. Companies can make direct sales to the private sector from outside Saudi Arabia. However, appointing an agent or distributor is the most common procedure for companies wishing to enter the Saudi market.

Virtually all government purchasing is conducted by local tenders and in the majority of cases only Saudi Arabian companies may bid. Foreign companies need a Saudi agent to bid for Saudi government tenders. The relationship between a foreign contractor and his Saudi agent is regulated by the Ministry of Commerce.

Exclusivity

Saudi Law permits the appointment of more than one agent on a regional basis, and for particular products. Many companies, however, prefer to appoint a sole agent to avoid conflict of interest and possible mix-up especially when bidding for Government contracts

Language

Arabic is the official language, although English is widely used in the main towns and is the main business language.

Chapter 17: Railway Sector Opportunities in Saudi Arabia

Saudi Arabia is presently investing over US$45 billion to develop its world class rail networks. Its ambition of a better and bigger railway is starting to come into life, with its new railway projects covering a total length of 7,000 km.

The allocated budget for rail development in KSA is believed to be $90bn over 30 years. This 30 year master plan will provide 'an integrated and clear future vision' for a 'safer, better and bigger railway. The projects already announced and in progress are:

1. US $ 7.5bn - Jeddah-Riyadh, Dammam-Jubail Railway - (Landbridge) project.

2. US $ 12.3 bn - Haramain High Speed Rail Link - a 444 kilo meters high-speed track that will link the Muslim holy cities of Medinah and Makkah via King Abdullah Economic City, Rabigh, Jeddah and King Abdulaziz International Airport. Project in progress.

3. US$ 2.3 bn - Ras ALZour (Ras Al Khair)-Jubail-Dammam Rail Link Project.

4. US $ 25 bn Gulf Cooperation Council (GCC) Rail Project.

5. Extending from Saudi Arabia to Kuwait, Qatar, Bahrain, UAE and Muscat.

6. US $ 20 bn - Urban Mass Rail Transit System - Makkah Metro, a project of 182 km with 88 stations, to link different areas of Holy Makkah with the Grand Mosque.

7. US $ 7-8bn Riyadh Metro: Arriyadh Development Authority (ADA) has issued invitation for contractors to prequalify for the main construction package on the planned $7-8bn Riyadh metro project before 20 June 2012.

Riyadh metro project invited global consortia, specialised in production and supply of rolling stocks, controls, telecommunications systems, as well as metro tunnelling, civil, mechanical and electrical works, to pre-qualify for the main construction package on the planned $7-8bn Riyadh metro project before 20 June 2012.

Saudi Railway Company (SAR) is inviting companies to submit bids by 26 May for the contract to carry out detailed engineering design for the kingdom's planned $7.5 bn Landbridge rail project.

Saudi Arabia's experience in the railway industry is relatively new and could be described as modest compared with the UK. There is only one small railway (400 km) in the country. Railway manufacturing is not well established in Saudi Arabia. Saudi Railways Organisation (SRO) operates and maintains the current network and welcomes foreign expertise. They have imported rail engines, carriages, rail track, sleepers, etc from USA, Switzerland, France, Korea, etc.

To maintain its reputation as a provider of good and reliable service, SRO is keen to improve standards of their operation. Thus, there is ongoing requirement for material/equipment suppliers and service providers in the sector.

All materials and equipment used in Saudi Rail projects are to be approved by the Saudi Railway Organisation. Quality and technical standards are more important than price in bid decisions.

Adherence to schedules and specifications and long-term commitment for after sales service are key, to win projects. Business tends to be done through direct procurement rather than via agents. Technical and regulatory standards in Saudi Arabia are different to those of the EU, hence should be well studied and understood.

Foreign companies are advised to familiarise themselves with sample specifications at the earliest opportunity.

Chapter 18: Healthcare Opportunities in Saudi Arabia

Healthcare in Saudi Arabia continues to be a thriving sector as the government seeks to finance health services for a rapidly growing population of 28 million. It is the largest market for medical equipment and healthcare products in the Gulf and Middle East.

The Kingdom of Saudi Arabia is a market where good opportunities exist and where UK companies can succeed. The Kingdom is the UK's 23rd largest export market worth £1.6 billion (£1=SR6.17 approx). It is one of the UK's largest trading partners in the Middle East and largest export market in the region. The UK is Saudi Arabia's 2nd largest joint investor overall.

Saudi healthcare market is classified into three broad segments:
1. Ministry of Health.
2. Non-Ministry of Health (military, National Guard, security forces, university hospitals etc).
3. Private.

Each of these segments bears their own distinctive characteristics.

Healthcare Infrastructure

The Saudi Government announced its 2012 budget of SR690 billion ($172.5 billion), a projected surplus of SR12 billion ($3 billion). 2012 will be the fourth consecutive year that economic growth will be heavily dependent on Saudi government spending.

The government's priorities are education which was allocated the biggest share followed by transport and "health and social affairs" receiving the largest increase in their allocations.

As seen in recent years, health and social affairs was awarded a 26 percent rise in its budget i.e. SR86.5 billion which is a 26% rise over last year. New projects will include 17 new hospitals and new primary care centres throughout the Kingdom. At present there are more than 130 hospitals under various stages of planning and construction with a capacity of 28,470 beds. The new budget includes appropriation to build sport clubs, social centres, social, welfare and labour offices.

The Higher Education Ministry has also announced plans to establish medical colleges and hospitals at all of the Kingdom's 24 government universities. They have already started work on some of the university hospitals and contracts will be awarded soon to implement the rest of the university hospital projects. These educational hospitals will also provide health services to people in their respective provinces.

Special Needs

Saudi Arabia has also established an efficient network of facilities to treat and rehabilitate the mentally and physically handicapped. The Ministry of Health and the Ministry of Labour and Social Affairs have established a network of rehabilitation centres for the handicapped. These facilities fall into two categories. The first offers services for medical, physical and mental treatment and rehabilitation of patients and is operated or supervised by the Ministry of Health. There are currently 18 such centres. The second group of centres focuses on the social rehabilitation of the handicapped and is run by the Ministry of Labour and Social Affairs. There are presently 14 centres throughout the country that teach the mentally and physically impaired social, educational and vocational skills designed to help them enter society as independent, productive individuals.

There are also 24 special education institutes for the blind and the deaf in Saudi Arabia and three centres for handicapped children. The special needs (handicapped) market is a largely untapped market and offers great potential to those overseas suppliers who are willing to invest in providing training on their products.

Medical Training

The Kingdom has been spending generously in the field of medical training and plans to further improve medical education to ensure medical students are kept abreast of the latest developments. According to the latest available figures, there are now almost 5100 male and female students attending the Kingdom's medical colleges and a further 2300 students are studying medicine abroad.

The government and some private hospitals have announced plans for opening new medical colleges and universities. The ones to be established by the private sector will require Government approval.

Dentistry

There are more than 107 dental facilities at Government hospitals including specialised dental hospitals and around 320 private dental clinics. The private dental clinics are increasing with the growing awareness of oral hygiene. In addition to some others the British Centres for Excellence in Dentistry, London has set up a specialised clinic in Riyadh in collaboration with the Saudi British Hospital. These and other dental clinics are creating opportunities for suppliers of cosmetics, consumables, tools and dental equipment.

Health Insurance

The government is working on expanding the health insurance sector, which in 2009, was valued at around SR5 billion (£ 0.9 billion). This is expected to increase to SR7 billion (£1.2 billion) in the short term with new regulations introduced in January 2009 to expand the insurance scheme to Saudi nationals working in small and medium enterprises in the private sector.

The large private sector companies already provide health insurance for their employers.

Medical Products

In 2007, the Saudi government established the National Company for Unified Purchase of Medicines and Medical Appliances, to act as the sole supplier of medicines and medical appliances to government health institutions. The company was set up to bring down the prices of medical devices and pharmaceuticals by preventing overcharging. The company is in its early phase and developing coordination with other stake holders like SGH executive Board and hospitals.

The Saudi Food & Drug Authority (SFDA) have been given the task of developing and enforcing a regulatory system for medical devices. This will include establishing licensing procedures for manufacturers and suppliers. In what is a first step in developing a regulatory framework for medical devices, the SFDA in 2007 started the Medical Devices National Registry (MDNR), which will become a mandatory web-based project involving the registration of manufacturers, agents and suppliers in the country. From July 2009 all regulatory responsibilities were handed over to SFDA for pharmaceuticals, medical devices and food.

It is now mandatory for local distributors / agents to register and obtain MDEL (Medical Device Establishment License) and all overseas suppliers to register their company and products with the SFDA.

US FDA, Canadian, European, Japanese and Australian certification are acceptable for product registration under MDNR. Manufacturers can register themselves and their products either directly or through their local agent/distributors.

Pharmaceuticals

According to market sources, imported pharmaceuticals account for around 82 percent of the market with little manufacturing being undertaken locally. Generic medicines make up approx 5.8 percent of the market share. With the Saudi pharmaceutical market worth approx. £2.6 billion in 2009, market analysts forecast that import of medicines will continue to keep climbing in Saudi Arabia as it is the largest consuming market in the GCC.

The pharmaceuticals manufacturing industry continues to expand moderately with seven local manufacturers producing a range of generic pharmaceuticals and co-marketing with multi-national companies. They supply around 10 percent of the total medicines market. The balance is imported from the US and Europe but for the last few years generic brands are being imported from the neighbouring Gulf countries, Egypt and Jordan. The MOH remains the single largest customer for pharmaceuticals in the Kingdom with annual purchases of approximately £150 million with the balance being purchased by GCC tenders, non-MOH government hospitals, private hospitals and pharmacies.

Accreditation

The rapidly increasing demand for health services has created renewed concerns for the government. So as to lessen the burden on their budget, some MOH and non-MOH government hospitals have started business centres, where private patients, irrespective of their entitlements can get treatment by paying for such services. With the expansion of healthcare insurance coverage the government is looking at the possibility of leasing out government hospitals to private sector in the future, as almost all the population by that time will be covered by insurance.

The Government is considering plans to ask Saudi hospitals to adhere to quality standards by implementing quality improvement at hospitals and some Canadian and US companies are working with the Saudi MOH on implementation and training of evaluators for inspecting the hospitals and providing accreditation.

Medical Equipment and Supplies

Market sources valued the medical equipment and supplies market in the Kingdom at £250 million in 2006, predominantly supplied through imports. Of this figure 69% accounted for medical equipment. This is expected to grow to £400 million by 2015. German, US and Japanese companies lead in the export of large medical equipment to the Kingdom whilst the small to medium size equipment is supplied mostly by the US, Germany, UK, Japan and other European suppliers.

Chapter 19: Environment Opportunities in Saudi Arabia

The Saudi Presidency of Meteorology and Environment (PME) now have new environmental legislation, and the Implementation Procedures of this legislation endorsed by the Government. New environmental standards have also been re-written, and the PME is now strictly ensuring implementation of legislation and standards. Environmental Inspectors have been recruited by the PME and Green Police is on its way to be formed. This new legislation, standards and enforcement procedures have now become drivers for improved environmental performance and business in the country.

The Government has allocated US$300 million for environmental protection and pollution control in the current budget. In addition, a substantial amount of the US$3 billion budget for the Ministry of Municipality and Housing has been set aside for the handling, processing, managing and disposal of solid waste.

"According to the World Bank, Saudi Arabia will have to invest about US$20 billion in its environmental sector over the next 10 years in order to ensure a safer environment."

The following areas offer potential business opportunities in the sector:

Environmental Impact Assessment (EIA)

All new major industrial projects in the Kingdom now require an Environmental Impact Assessment at the planning and feasibility study stage, without which a license will not be issued.

Wastewater

There is severe lack of expertise in the field of wastewater treatment, which has led to a marked increase in water pollution in the Kingdom.

Wastewater collection and treatment systems exist in only 22 out of 106 Municipal areas, and some major towns and cities have no piped collection systems as yet. It is estimated that of all the wastewater collected, only one third is to the tertiary standards required by regulation for reuse. Many of the existing plants are obsolete and need rehabilitation.

A major construction programme of wastewater treatment plants is needed to increase capacity. A study by the Ministry of Water and Electricity estimates that Saudi Arabia will need to invest about US$20 Billion for building new sewer networks and about US$17Billion on new waste treatment plants over the next 20 years.

Waste disposal

Studies show that the average weight of domestic/home solid waste per individual in Saudi Arabia is expected to rise to 1.2Kg/day by 2010.

There is a desperate need in the Kingdom for new technologies and techniques for handling this waste. Little or no recycling currently takes place. There is also a major requirement for latest incineration technologies. Domestic, industrial, chemical and hazardous waste is on the increase in Saudi Arabia, thanks to the country's industrialization and urban growth.

Organic waste represents the highest percentage of domestic municipal waste collected (40%), followed by paper and cartons (20%), plastic (15%), metal (7%), glass (5%), clothes (4%), and other waste (9%). Saudi Arabia generates also about 25,000 tons of medical hazardous waste per year. The Government approved the establishment of a joint stock company to treat hazardous waste in the country, under the Ministry of Health.

Destruction of toxic and isotropic waste produced by factories is problematic. The Government is trying to tackle the negative impact of industrial waste, especially those containing lead and radium. Random collection and burning of industrial waste is widespread and leads to emission of poisonous gases and air pollutants.

With over 1,200 factories in the country, and little environmental awareness, Saudi Arabia offers enormous potential business to UK companies in this sector. A new Law announced in July 2005 makes it now mandatory for companies executing industrial and commercial projects to install surveillance equipment to monitor pollution. The Law also envisages installing surveillance equipment in different parts of the country to detect offenders.

Air Pollution

According to the Municipal and Rural Affairs Ministry, Saudi air pollution is on the increase. Saudi Aramco, the Saudi oil giant, operates 10 Air Quality Monitoring and Meteorology Network (AMMNET) stations and 15 meteorology-only stations throughout the country. AMMNET stations ensure facilities meet national and company air quality standards for limits of sulphur dioxide, inhalable particulates, ozone, nitrogen oxides, carbon monoxide and hydrogen sulphide, among other pollutants. The PME also has a number of these stations installed at the country's airports, the industrial cities of Jubail and Yanbu, and elsewhere. More will be installed soon.

Saudi annual imports of air pollution control and monitoring equipment at the moment stands at about U\$50 Million. Sources expect an average annual growth of 7% in this sector brought about primarily by new mega projects in the petrochemical field, oil and gas, power generation and water desalination industries. Pollutants emitted by thermal power plants in Saudi Arabia cost the national economy about US\$2 billion a year.

Local companies lack the know-how in specialised areas of pollution control, such as:
1. Environmental monitoring.
2. Environmental analytical services.
3. Environmental engineering & consultancy.

4. Hazardous waste management.
5. Site remediation and rehabilitation.

Marine Pollution

According to a recent independent study, the Arabian Gulf marine pollution constitutes about 30% of the World's oil pollution. Oil tanker movement is the main cause.

Other opportunities

Opportunities also exist in ambient surveys, air quality surveys, and emission source testing for gases and particulate. The country also has 9 large cement factories that emit large amounts of dust to the atmosphere. New regulations require these factories to develop electrostatic precipitation techniques to reduce air pollution. Remote controlled monitoring devices, environmental monitoring stations, oil spill cleaning works and environmental laboratories are also in high demand.

The Saudi government has also intensified its efforts to increase public awareness and encourage individual and group initiatives to protect the environment.

Chapter 20: Conclusion

Saudi Arabia is an absolute monarchy, although, according to the Basic Law of Saudi Arabia adopted by royal decree in 1992, the king must comply with Sharia (that is, Islamic law) and the Quran. The Quran and the Sunnah (the traditions of Muhammad) are declared to be the country's constitution, but no written modern constitution has ever been written for Saudi Arabia, and Saudi Arabia remains the only Arab Nation where no national elections have ever taken place, since its creation. No political parties or national elections are permitted and according to The Economist's 2010 Democracy Index, the Saudi government is the seventh most authoritarian regime from among the 167 countries rated.

On 25 September 2011, Saudi Arabia's King Abdullah has announced that women will have the right to stand and vote in future local elections and join the advisory Shura council as full member and be able to run as candidates in the municipal election.

People in Saudi Arabia respect their culture and uphold their tradition. They follow the dictates of the Quran and consider it to be their book of guidelines. For foreigner there are certain basic Do's and Don'ts in Saudi Arabia that shall make your stay a success.

According to the Quran consumption of alcohol is forbidden. Eating of pork too is prohibited. Foreigners therefore cannot indulge in drinks and in all the international restaurants there is no provision of a bar. The menu also does not consist of cuisine made of pork. Tobacco consumption is also not a very acceptable practice. Foreigners should stick to these restrictions to avoid any problems.

The Saudi Arabian Customs and Traditions state that on friendly and formal meets guests should be offered black tea as a sign of cordiality. So when you visit local households they should drink a cup of tea to acknowledge the hospitality of the housemates. Saudi Arabian tradition also stresses on dress codes of the men and women.

Each person customarily wears long flowing and loose garments. This is in accord of the hijab custom that insists on the maintenance of modesty. Usually men wear an ankle length cotton shirt called thwab. It is accompanied by either a check-shirt which is known as the keffiyeh or a ghutra. For women it is compulsory to wear a niquab, that is, a veil.

Good luck!

Part 3: CEO Guide to Doing Business in Kuwait

Chapter 21: Introduction

The land area of Kuwait is about 17,818 square kilometres, or roughly the size of Wales. Kuwait is a closely-knit society, the people are well educated and many speak English fluently.

Kuwait's economy is heavily dependent on oil revenues. The Kuwait government is keen on reducing the dependence on crude oil revenue. It plans to increase investment in downstream industries of the oil sector and also through promoting the role of the private sector and privatisation.

Kuwaitis are fine negotiators. Its merchants have a reputation for financial astuteness and business acumen.

Today's Kuwaiti businessmen, many of whom have been educated in Europe or the US, have considerable experience of the business methods of both East and West, and their shrewdness should never be underestimated.

Strengths of the market
1. Kuwait has 10% of the world's oil reserves.
2. Kuwait has the most advanced democracy in comparison to its gulf neighbours and Kuwaitis are proud of it.
3. In 2009, four female MPs were elected for the first time.
4. Kuwait is one of the single largest investors in the UK in terms of liquidity, investment

portfolios and property, both by Government institutions, private sector companies and private individuals.

5. Kuwait is a major buyer of British military equipment and training. As well as security services.

Opportunities in Kuwait

Kuwait in 2010 is in line for a recovery from a tricky but not difficult 2009. The impact from Dubai should be limited. Building on higher oil prices and a need to improve infrastructure will drive business. Kuwait's Development Plan, announced late 2009, aims to transform Kuwait from an oil dependant country into a commercial and financial hub. Oil prices between $75-100 provides the means to finance ambitious new investment. The 2009-2010 surplus is estimated to be over £15 billion. Thanks largely to high oil prices, but also burgeoning financial and logistics sectors, GDP rose to over $148 billion or rather more than $50,000 per capita in 2008. However Kuwait will need to overcome internal political disputes to realise its potential.

Chapter 22: Kuwaiti Society and Culture

Language in Kuwait

Arabic is the official language of Kuwait, but English is widely spoken. It is used in business and is a compulsory second language in schools. Among the non-Kuwaiti population, many people speak Farsi, the official language of Iran, or Urdu, the official language of Pakistan.

Arabic is spoken by almost 200 million people in more than 22 countries. It is the language of the Qur'an, the Holy Book of Islam, and of Arab poetry and literature. While spoken Arabic varies from country to country, classical Arabic has remained unchanged for centuries. In Kuwait, there are differences between the dialects spoken in urban areas and those spoken in rural areas.

Islam

Islam is practised by the majority of Kuwaitis and governs their personal, political, economic and legal lives. Islam emanated from what is today Saudi Arabia. The Prophet Muhammad is seen as the last of God's emissaries (following in the footsteps of Jesus, Moses, Abraham, etc) to bring revelation to mankind. He was distinguished with bringing a message for the whole of mankind, rather than just to a certain peoples. As Moses brought the Torah and Jesus the

Bible, Muhammad brought the last book, the Quran. The Quran and the actions of the Prophet (the Sunnah) are used as the basis for all guidance in the religion.

Among certain obligations for Muslims are to pray five times a day at dawn, noon, afternoon, sunset, and evening. The exact time is listed in the local newspaper each day. Friday is the Muslim holy day. Everything is closed. Many companies also close on Thursday, making the weekend Thursday and Friday.

During the holy month of Ramadan all Muslims must fast from dawn to dusk and are only permitted to work six hours per day. Fasting includes no eating, drinking, cigarette smoking, or gum chewing. Expatriates are not required to fast; however, they must not eat, drink, smoke, or chew gum in public.

Each night at sunset, families and friends gather together to celebrate the breaking of the fast (iftar). The festivities often continue well into the night. In general, things happen more slowly during Ramadan. Many businesses operate on a reduced schedule. Shops may be open and closed at unusual times.

Although over 95% of the population are Muslim, Kuwait is known for its religious tolerance. The three Churches are allowed to practice freely. Kuwait is the only Gulf Country to establish relations with the Vatican.

Family Values

The extended family is the basis of the social structure and individual identity. It includes the nuclear family, immediate relatives, distant relatives, tribe members, friends, and neighbours.

Nepotism is viewed positively, since it guarantees hiring people who can be trusted, which is crucial in a country where working with people one knows and trusts is of primary importance.

The family is private. Female relatives are protected from outside influences. It is considered inappropriate to ask questions about a Kuwaiti's wife or other female relatives.

Chapter 23: Business Etiquette and Protocol in Kuwait

Meeting Etiquette

Kuwaitis are hospitable; however, it is important to behave according to their cultural norms. Although women play a greater role in Kuwaiti society than women do in many other Gulf countries, they seldom socialize together in public.

Greetings are therefore between members of the same sex. In all cases they are given with a sense of enthusiasm and general pleasure at meeting or seeing the person again. Kuwaitis take time during the greeting process to converse about their health, family, mutual friends and acquaintances, and other general matters of interest.

Naming Conventions

The first name is the personal name and used as we would use ours. The second name is the father's personal name. It is used with the connector "al- ". The third and fourth names are the grandfather's personal name and a name that denotes the family lineage. Both names generally start with the prefix "al- ". The name of Suleyman Al-Ahmed Al- Mustafa Al-Sabah means Suleyman, son of Ahmed, grandson of Mustafa of the Sabah family/tribe. Women do not take the husband's name upon marriage.

Gift Giving Etiquette

Extended family or very close friends may exchange gifts for birthdays, Ramadan, Eid, Hajj and other celebratory occasions. If you are invited to a Kuwaiti home, bring a houseplant, box of imported chocolates, or a small gift from your home country.

If a man must give a gift to a woman, he should say that it is from his wife, mother, sister, or some other female relative. Do not give alcohol unless you know for sure he/she partakes. Gifts are not opened when received.

Dining Etiquette

Kuwaitis socialize in their homes, restaurants, or international hotels. If both sexes are included, they may be entertained in separate rooms, although this is not always the case.

When going to a Kuwaitis house

Check to see if the host is wearing shoes. If not, remove yours at the door. Dress conservatively. Show respect for the elders by greeting them first. Accept any offer of food or drink. To turn down hospitality is to reject the person. If you are invited for a meal, there is often a great deal of socializing and small talk before the meal and the evening comes to an end quickly after the meal.

Watch your table manners!

Eat only with the right hand. Meals are generally served family-style. Guests are served first. Then the oldest, continuing in some rough approximation of age order until the youngest is served. Honoured guests are often offered the most prized pieces or delicacies such as the sheep's head - so be prepared!

Hospitality and generosity dictate showering guests with abundance. Leave some food on your plate when you have finished eating otherwise they will fill it with more. When the host stands, the meal is over.

Relationships and Communication

Since Kuwaitis prefer to do business with those with whom they have a personal relationship, they spend a great deal of time on the getting-to-know-you process. You must be patient since impatience is viewed as criticism of the culture. Kuwaitis judge on appearances so dress and present yourself well. They respect education, so carefully mention if you have an advanced degree, especially if it is from a prestigious university.

Business Meeting Etiquette

Try to schedule meetings in the morning when meeting with government officials, since they are restricted to a 6-hour day. Many businessmen prefer to meet in the early evening. Do not try to schedule meetings in July and August as many Kuwaitis leave the country during the worst of the summer heat.

Meetings may be interrupted if they interfere with prayer times. Meetings are generally not private unless there is a need to discuss matters confidentially. Expect frequent interruptions. Others may wander into the room and start a different discussion. You may join in, but do not try to bring the topic back to the original discussion until the new person leaves.

Business Negotiating

Business will only be discussed once an atmosphere of trust and friendship has been established. Kuwaitis are event rather than time-driven. The event of getting together is more important than the timeliness of the meeting or the outcome. Kuwait is a hierarchical society. Many companies are structured around the family. Decisions usually come from the top after determining a consensus of the various stakeholders. Decisions are reached slowly. If you try to rush things, you will give offence and risk your business relationship.

Kuwaitis are shrewd negotiators who are especially interested in price. Do not use high-pressure sales tactics. They will work against you. Repeating your main points indicates you are telling the truth. There is a tendency to avoid giving bad news and to give flowery acceptances, which may only mean "perhaps". Problems may be discussed outside the meeting in a one-on-one situation rather than in the group meeting room.

If you change the lead negotiator, negotiations will need to start over. Proposals and contracts should be kept simple. Although negotiating is done in English, contracts are written in Arabic. If there is both an English and Arabic version, the Arabic will be the one followed.

Dress Etiquette

Business attire is conservative. Men should wear lightweight, good quality, conservative suits, at least to the initial meeting. Women should avoid giving offence and refrain from wearing revealing or tight fitting clothing. Although they do not need to wear skirts that reach the ground, skirts should cover the knee and sleeves should cover the elbow and fasten at the neck.

Titles

Titles are important. Use the honorific "Mister" and any academic or political title and the first name. Do not use only the first name until expressly invited to drop the titles. The title "Sheikh" denotes that someone is a member of the royal family. It is also used for old men.

Business Cards

Business cards are given to everyone you meet. Have one side of your card translated into Arabic. Be sure to check the translation carefully as there is often confusion with the order of western names.

Chapter 24: Opportunities in Kuwait

Oil & Gas

In the oil and gas sector the government are looking to invest £50b in new projects. Kuwait is looking to increase its capacity of crude oil to 4 million barrels a day by 2020.

There are also plans and projects, which are underway to expand and upgrade existing facilities. There are a number of downstream projects including a 4th refinery. Shell is developing Kuwait's Northern Gas reserves.

Project Kuwait, a plan to bring in the IOC's to boost production in the northern fields has remained mired in politics, but the work is instead being carried out by the Kuwait Oil Company and managed by firms such as AMEC, Fluor and Petrofac who have won very significant business.

Downstream, upgraded export facilities, a fourth (615,000 bpd) refinery and two new petrochemical plants are planned. At current prices, well over US$60 billion is due to be spent in the sector by 2020.

Financial Services

The Kuwaiti financial system is sizeable and well developed. Besides commercial and specialized banks at the core of the system, it includes a growing number of financial companies and investment funds, as well as insurance companies and an active stock exchange. Although the establishment of new banks domestically is restricted, there is adequate competition and opportunities in financial markets, with the exception of the insurance sector. Domestic institutions offer a wide range of up-to-date services.

Construction

With multi-billion dollar budget surplus for 2009, the government is expected to embark on a number of projects. The government is looking to fund/implement several large-scale developments. It is estimated that projects worth over £130 billion are planned, including the high profile development of island projects – Failaka and Bubiyan. Others include expansion of Kuwait Airport, extension of existing Ring Roads and the construction of an 8th Ring Road. Renovation and development of sewerage network, building of Subiya causeway, a metro rail system and utility plants are also being planned. Additionally, new city developments in Subiya, Khairan, Jaber Al Ahmed city, Arifjan and other smaller satellite city developments such as Al Mutlaa, Saad Al Abdullah, and Sabah Al Ahmad city are likely to provide further opportunities for foreign industries.

The government is looking to fund a number of projects for the development of northern bay of Kuwait. This plan includes the construction of Silk City, which is estimated to over £55b, a road and rail network and a new Bubiyan Port and housing projects. A cornerstone of the programme is Silk City, a planned financial and commercial hub which will be located in Subiya.

As a stimulant to the project is the Bubiyan Port Project which when completed will boast of a modern port with the capability to fuel economic growth helping Kuwait to grow as a trading hub.

A new Kuwait University (University City) is being planned. It will provide a modern campus with state of the art facilities for academic staff, students and other employees of Kuwait University. It will include several faculties, dormitories, sports facilities and auditoriums as well as car parks for several thousand vehicles. There will also be a medical school and an associated 400-bed teaching hospital. The campus will cost about £4 billion over ten years.

Education and Training

Education is key to reform. In particular, the need for more skills-based learning, through better ICT, to increase the employability of Kuwaiti youth across the private sector. Kuwait's draft education strategy demonstrates a commitment to developing a modern, qualitative and outward looking education strategy.

The current educational strategy includes 31 projects for all school levels to be implemented within the next four years, such as establishing an educational TV station, utilising personal computers, using white/active smart boards and other relevant

105

technologies. The Ministry through one of its departments, Kuwait Educational Development Centre, has set-up committees and teams to look into proposals to update the general goals of public education development and the 2005-2025 educational strategy. Their mission is to consider new educational developments, scientific studies and experiments which are being integrated in countries like the UK.

We believe that the educational sector will remain profitable within the coming years as the government is keen on improving the standard of education in Kuwait. The private sector too is forging ahead with new schools and even universities, the market for equipping these ran to some $300m last year.

Power

The country plans to invest billions in increasing power capacity to approximately 16 (GW) by 2012 from around 10 (GW) in 2008. Four power plants are planned to come on-line by 2013 to avert a power shortage.

Environment

Comprehensive studies on the solid waste sector in Kuwait including an assessment of the existing conditions and the identification of investment opportunities in waste recycling have been carried out. The current miss-management and poor disposal practices coupled with inefficient use of spare land are causing environmental, economic, social and health impacts. A number of investment opportunities are available in recycling activities, which include the establishment of integrated, cost effective and sustainable municipal solid waste management where both the private and public sector can jointly participate.

Aviation

Kuwait has already made significant investment in infrastructure to accommodate growth. The centrepiece of Kuwait's expansion plan is a £1.4 billion upgrade of Kuwait International Airport. Kuwait Airways, the country's national carrier is in the process of privatisation, while Kuwait's two low cost carriers continue with further expansion. Opportunities exist in Airport security, Air traffic management and training.

Healthcare

The nation's healthcare sector will benefit from the Governments development plans. The Kuwait government has plans for the construction of eight new hospitals, which are being planned to be open before 2017. There are also a number of healthcare service centres that will be opened. Currently the Jaber Ahmed Al Sabah Hospital costing over $1b is under construction.

Retail

Retail sales rose from £20b in 2008 to almost £33b in 2009. Among the factors that will stimulate growth are an increasing population in the 22 to 45 age bracket (and a high level of urbanisation with nearly 99% of those living in Kuwait expected to be residing in built up areas by 2015). High levels of disposable income have sustained consumer spending from which, through their franchised local stores, UK high street names such a Debenhams, Next, Mothercare, M&S and Boots have benefited, to the tune of some £250m last year. British goods dominate the market with high street brands such as M&S, Boots, Debenhams and Next being household names.

Defence and Security

Kuwait has major projects planned in both the defence and security sectors over the medium to long term. There is a significant budget for the replacement and upgrade of much of the Armed Forces inventory. The planning for a number of these programmes is moving forward and we predict that over the next 10 years some £9-10Bn will be available for these projects.

On security, many programmes are planned in both the government and civil sectors. The Ministry of Interior has a number of large scale projects it hopes to achieve; some of these are based around homeland and border security. In the quickly growing civil sector projects with security elements include the oil and gas sector and major construction projects such as Bubiyan Port. Kuwait is one of the few posts around the world with a specialist officer from UKTI Defence and Security Organisation at post to assist and advice on these prospects.

Chapter 25: Kuwait's Economic Overview

Kuwait is a small, rich, relatively open economy with self-reported crude oil reserves of about 104 billion barrels; 10% of world reserves. Petroleum accounts for nearly half of GDP, 95% of export revenues, and 80% of government income. Kuwait's climate limits agricultural development. Consequently, with the exception of fish, it depends almost wholly on food imports.

About 75% of potable water must be distilled or imported. High oil prices in recent years have helped build Kuwait's budget and trade surpluses and foreign reserves. As a result of this positive fiscal situation, the need for economic reforms is less urgent and the government has not earnestly pushed through new initiatives.

The majority of fiscal surpluses are transferred to the Kuwait Investment Authority (KIA), which manages the Reserve Fund for Future Generations (RFFG) and the General Reserve Fund (GRF). Details relating to the RFFG and GRF are not made public. However, in late June local media reported from a closed session of the parliament that total KIA assets rose 14% to KD 70.2 billion (£157 billion) at the end of March 2008 compared to a year earlier.

Its economic expansion continues to be fuelled by oil wealth, so much so that every sector of the economy has benefited from the profits attained through oil production.

Kuwait's GDP increased 176% between 2000 and 2006, with growth averaging 26% a year. However, these gains have also posed many new challenges. The government realises it must liberalise legislation regarding private enterprise, as well as control the rapid growth in credit and asset prices. In addition, it is vital that it begins developing Kuwait's non-oil sectors to ensure sustainability; a difficult task as oil revenues have been the catalyst for growth. Inflation has also caused concern for both the government and the central bank. Revaluing the dinar will serve to stem some of its growth, but this process is likely to be gradual.

Subsidies on electricity and key consumer goods have also helped to keep a lid on prices, but such subsidies are expected to rise in the coming year. To combat this, the government is considering the establishment of a price control committee to dissuade traders from hiking prices without approval. While many in Kuwait are able to absorb the rise in prices, the extensive, unskilled expatriate population, who a large part of the economy depends on, would be more vulnerable. Kuwait's efforts to create and strengthen ties with key economic players around the world are also beginning to pay off. Deals are currently in the works with Singapore, the US and the EU, while major contracts are already in place with Korea and China.

Population

The population of Kuwait has always been so small that the country has had to rely on foreign workers. Prior to the Iraqi invasion in 1990, nationals of virtually every country could be found working in Kuwait.

Membership of International Organisations

Kuwait became a member of the World Trade Organisation in 1995, and in 1997 the Kuwait National Assembly also ratified Kuwait's membership in the World Intellectual Property Organisation (WIPO).

A unified Patent Law is now in force for all member countries of the GCC, namely Bahrain, Kuwait, Oman, Qatar, Saudi Arabia and the United Arab Emirates. Applications must be sent to the GCC Patent office Riyadh, Saudi Arabia.

Trademarks may be registered for 10 years and renewed indefinitely for further 10 year periods. Registration takes about three weeks and a fee is payable. If a trademark has not been used for a five year period, an interested party can apply to have it cancelled.

Kuwait is not a party to any of the international conventions relating to copyright.

IP rights are territorial, i.e. they only give protection in the countries where they are granted or registered.

If you are thinking about trading internationally then you should consider registering your IP rights abroad.

Procurement processes

Although Arabic is the official language, English is widely used and spoken. Many Kuwaiti's speak English fluently as there are lots of private English and American schools and universities where all subject are taught in English and Arabic is taken as a subject.

You should understand that his first few contacts with a Kuwaiti firm may well be conducted with an expatriate or a non Kuwaiti Arab - a Lebanese, Egyptian or Palestinian, or a trusted Indian or Pakistani office Manager. In most Kuwaiti companies, the visiting businessman will have to work his way up and through the levels of assistant managers before meeting a decision-maker.

Traditional courtesy dictates that, even at the lowest level of the company, you will be met with goodwill. This can be frustrating if the company very quickly decides that your product is not for them, because few Arab managers will give you an abrupt rejection. Foreigners unfamiliar with local business methods may therefore still have the impression that clinching the deal is only a day away, when, in reality they are receiving a polite brush-off.

The golden rule is only talk business with a decision-maker. However, it is important to remain polite and courteous with all office staff. Careless remarks or a display of impatience will naturally be frowned on and will certainly reach the ears of senior management. The moment you step into an office you are under observation.

Kuwait's deep-rooted trading traditions earned its merchants a reputation for financial astuteness and business acumen long before the discovery of oil. Today's Kuwaiti businessmen, many of whom have been educated in Europe or the US, have considerable experience of the business methods of both East and West, and their shrewdness should never be underestimated.

The aggressive, hard sell does not appeal to Kuwaitis. Patience, small talk, low-key presentation, the desktop video tape of the product, samples and specimens, an attractive company brochure - these are not, as might be thought, cosmetic trimmings but an essential part of business behaviour.

Although negotiating is done in English, contracts are written in Arabic. If there is both an English and Arabic version, the Arabic will be the one followed. Business will only be discussed once an atmosphere of trust and friendship has been established. Do not seem in a hurry, do not talk of planes to catch and do not fret over a taxi back to the hotel (the client can probably arrange for a car to take you back). Kuwaitis expect punctuality, but your schedule should allow you flexibility in case of any delay on their part. All local telephone calls are free of charge, and most shopkeepers or office staff will be happy to let you use their telephones to confirm a company's location or leave a message that you will be late for an appointment.

Procurement processes might appear bureaucratic, but the situation is demonstrably improving. There are some concerns regarding slow release of bonds, although indications are that these are mostly justified. Bid and performance bonds are now centrally agreed with current rates of 2.5 per cent for bid bonds and 10 per cent for performance bonds being applied in line with regional levels, to attract more international engagement. Some payment delays have been experienced, but recent changes in legislation (supported by high oil prices) have minimised such instances and rarely is official intervention required. Kuwait ratified the UN Convention against Corruption in 2007, adopted a National anti-corruption strategy in 2008 and in March 2011 a series of new draft laws were presented to establish a national anti-corruption authority. All the signs are that these issues are being addressed at the highest level.

Commitment

Kuwait, as all other Gulf States, places great emphasis on trust and the importance of the family. It is therefore imperative that foreign companies understand and consider local culture and expectations when seeking business in Kuwait, especially the importance of forming strong personal relationships with potential partners and procurement bodies, long before business is sought. Kuwaiti buyers prefer proposals from individuals (not always companies) who they know and trust. The relationship-building process takes time and it is not unusual that several market visits are required before this level of trust can be attained. More positively, once a relationship is formed, business growth will be rapid, and the personal bonds formed is not easily forgotten.

Collaborative working

To achieve the ambitious objectives of such an aggressive and short-term development programme, the Kuwaiti Government will require significant levels of international company engagement and will focus on packaged solutions to deliver major and complex projects. The UK reputation for quality and robustness is highly regarded but is often outweighed by packaged/consortia proposals from elsewhere. It is clear that UK companies must be more willing to co-operate together and deliver solutions to complex developments.

The Kuwait market presents foreign businesses, large and small, with genuine opportunities for engagement in a diverse range of sectors. Continuing higher than expected oil revenues enhance their already strong financial position, suggesting the ambitious national development plan will undoubtedly succeed.

Kuwaiti buyers and officials regularly indicate that businesses from the UK are seen as their favoured partners, and the large number of UK professional services companies already active in Kuwait indicates the important role played by the UK. Commitment is the key to the development of successful business relations in Kuwait, and UK companies should be prepared to demonstrate commitment to Kuwait if the ambition to become "partners of choice" is to be achieved.

Chapter 26: Kuwait's Political Overview

The State of Kuwait is a Constitutional emirate whose Head of State is the Amir, His Highness Sheikh Sabah Al Ahmed Al Jaber Al Sabah, who acceded in February 2006.

Succession is hereditary and restricted to the ruling Al Sabah family. The Amir is aided by the Crown Prince, HE Sheikh Nawaf Al Ahmed Al Jaber Al Sabah, and the Council of Ministers, headed by the Prime Minister, HE Sheikh Nasser Mohammed Al Ahmed Al Sabah who is the head of the government. Power is exercised by the Amir through a Council of Ministers headed by a Prime Minister chosen by the Amir.

Legislative power is shared between the Amir and an elected National Assembly, whose members serve a four-year term and drawn from the Kuwaiti population.

Kuwait has a National Assembly of 50 elected members (who are elected freely by secret ballot) plus 15 cabinet ministers. The National Assembly can act freely and criticise the Cabinet, but the Amir retains the right to overrule the Assembly and can dissolve Parliament, and has exercised this right on several occasions. Legislation must be sanctioned by the head of government and can be initiated by the Amir, the Ministers, or the National Assembly.

Kuwait is a member of the six-country Gulf Co-operation Council (GCC) as well as of the Organisation of Petroleum Exporting Countries (OPEC).

Greater adoption of GCC-wide standards is expected in the future, especially after the establishment of the customs union in March 2005. Starting from 2008, citizens from Kuwait, Bahrain, Qatar, Oman, Saudi Arabia and UAE have equal rights to carry out business in any GCC country. This would include residency rights, working in government and private institutions, real estate ownership and investment opportunities, move freely within the GCC and receive education and healthcare benefits.

The aim of the Gulf common market is to create one market, raising production efficiency, optimum usage of available resources and improving the six countries negotiating position among international economic forums.

Chapter 27: Market Entry and Start-up Considerations

In most cases doing business in Kuwait requires local representation in the form of an agent or distributor.

The appointment of a local partner/representative will only be the first step. Kuwait is a market in which family structures predominate in the business environment, and where personal relationships therefore are important. This requires an investment primarily of time and personal presence. Likewise, product training for the agent's workforce is essential, as are regular updates on developments, modifications, competitor activity etc. Therefore regular visits to the market, especially during the early phase, are an important part of a successful interaction with the agent/distributor.

Foreign companies wishing to operate in Kuwait without setting up a Kuwaiti registered legal entity may only do so through a Kuwaiti agent. Establishing new business works best with a carefully chosen Kuwaiti partner or advisor, who is able to keep in contact with customers, seek business and provide information on the latest market trends. The success of the relationship with the agent depends upon face-to-face contact and regular communication. Companies providing promotional and marketing assistance to their agent will have an advantage.

Kuwait has a number of industrial areas, the largest being located in Shuwaikh, Sabhan and Shuaiba. Kuwait has its Free Trade Zone located at Shuwaikh port, under the supervision of Ministry of Commerce and Industry. The zone provides facilities for the storage and processing of goods, materials and other related activities, with companies operating there enjoying exemptions from all custom duties as well as streamlined visa procedures.

The basic laws regulating conducting business in Kuwait states that non-Kuwaitis cannot engage in commercial activities without a Kuwaiti partner whose equity holding should not be less than 51 per cent. An exception to this under Law No 8/2001 has been enacted permitting foreign entities to establish Kuwaiti companies with stakes up to 100% foreign equity participation.

The following ways define how a foreign individual or entity may enter the market and carry out business in Kuwait:
1. Establishing a company.
2. Signing a joint venture agreement.
3. Appointing a Kuwaiti commercial agent.
4. Appointing a commercial representative.
5. Applying for license under foreign investment law.

Establishing Company in Kuwait

As per the Kuwaiti Law, foreign individuals or entities may establish presence in the state through the formation and investment in the following type of companies:

1. Limited Liability Company (WLL).
2. Closed Joint Stock Company (KSC Closed).
3. Joint Stock Company.

Establishing a Joint Venture

Article (56) of the Kuwait Companies law refers to joint ventures as joint venture companies. As stated in Article (59), joint venture companies do not have legal personalities. These companies may not conduct business in their own name. Although joint ventures are simple contracts that require no formal establishment procedures, there can be complicated and confusing forms for carrying out business. Often foreign entities do not understand the nature of joint ventures under Kuwaiti Law.

Commercial Agency

Commercial agencies in Kuwait are governed by Law No. (36) of 1964 on the Regulation of Commercial Agencies, and Articles (260-296) of the Kuwaiti Commercial Code. Article 1 of the Law No. (36) of 1964 states that a non-Kuwaiti cannot act as commercial agents in Kuwait. There must be a direct relationship between the Kuwaiti agent and the foreign principal. Article 2 of Law No. (36) stipulates that commercial agencies are not enforceable unless recorded in the Commercial Register.

Commercial Representatives

A commercial representative is a Kuwaiti individual or entity engaged by a foreign company to represent its business interests in Kuwait. The authority scope of a commercial representative is more limited than that granted to an agent. A commercial representative's fees may be paid as a fixed regular amount, a commission, or percentage of the profits.

License under Foreign Investment Law

The Foreign Investment Law (No. 8/2001) proposes to regulate foreign investments in Kuwait. Under the law it is intended to allow foreign investors to own up to 100% equity in Kuwaiti companies or ventures for special projects as determined by the Council of Ministers. Prior to the enactment of this law, foreign investors were subject to a ceiling of 49% (maximum) stipulated under the Law of Commerce No. 68 of 1980 and the Commercial Companies Law No. 15 of 1960. The law proposes to do away with such restrictions imposed upon foreign investors.

Chapter 28: Customs and Regulations in Kuwait

Tariffs are based on the Harmonised International System (HIS) Code for classification of imports and exports.

Import tariffs in Kuwait are relatively low. A flat rate of 5% is applied to the cost, including insurance and freight of imported goods. Staple foods including rice, wheat and tea are exempt from import duties. Import duties on tobacco are 100% and could be increased in the near future.

Legislation and Local Regulations

Foreign corporate operations in Kuwait are liable to taxation on profits. The Kuwait Government has set a flat rate of 15 per cent which will be levied on the income of any foreign corporate carrying on trade or business in Kuwait.

A Double Taxation Agreement has been signed between the UK and Kuwait. For further details contact the Inland Revenue, International Division.

There is no personal income tax in Kuwait. The introduction of a sales tax has been discussed many times. It was scheduled for introduction for the fiscal year 1997/98 but this has yet to take place.

Responding to Tenders

The Central Tenders Committee (CTC), an independent government agency attached to the Council of Ministers, is the government authority responsible for prequalifying firms, issuing government tenders and awarding contracts. A limited number of government bodies and enterprises (Kuwait University, Kuwait Ports Authority and the Public Authority for Housing Care, Ministries of Defence and Interior) are exempt from CTC supervision and can issue tenders independently.

Consulting contracts do not fall under the purview of the CTC. Invitations to consultants are issued by the Consultants Selection Committee at the Ministry of Planning to the list of consultants registered with the Ministry.

A foreign company bidding for a government contract must be registered to operate in Kuwait and have a Kuwaiti agent. All government tenders, whether administered by the CTC or by another body are published in Al Kuwait Al Youm, the official gazette. Bids must be submitted to the CTC. A bid bond issued by a Kuwaiti bank of 2.5% to 5% of the value of the bid must be submitted with the bid.

Submitted tenders are evaluated on the basis of price and conformity to the technical specifications issued.

Pursuant to law number 19 (2000), any party awarded a direct contract by the public sector, including the military and oil sector bodies, must be in compliance with the minimum ratios for employment of Kuwaiti nationals as designated by the Council of Ministers.

Recruiting and Retaining Staffing

Recruitment consultants/agents play a major role in the placement of workers in a host of occupations in Kuwait. Kuwait has no equivalent of the nationally-organised job centres found in western countries due to which the Ministry of Labour and Social Affairs is responsible for all issues related to employment.

Kuwait is currently trying to balance the need for foreign labour with interests of its local population, and companies are strongly encouraged to hire local nationals wherever possible.

Documentation

An Arab-British Chamber of Commerce certificate of origin is required for all goods and can be obtained through an authorised British Chamber of Commerce.

Certificates of health are required for animals. Department for Environment, Food and Rural Affairs (DEFRA) certificates are required for foodstuffs. No particular format is prescribed for invoices. The declaration of origin should state "We hereby certify that the goods enumerated in this invoice are not of Israeli origin nor do they contain Israeli materials and are not being exported from Israel."

Invoices, certificates of origin and agreements must be certified by the Arab-British Chamber of Commerce or any British Chamber of Commerce and legalised by the Kuwaiti Embassy. Other documents must be authenticated at the Foreign and Commonwealth Office and legalised by the Kuwaiti Embassy. Fax signatures are accepted by customs.

A separate packing list must be provided unless the invoice contains all of the required information. British chambers of commerce are able to advise on the format of packing lists.

Labelling and Packaging Regulations

All imported goods must be labelled with the country of origin. Foodstuffs should have Arabic or Arabic/English labels and carry the following information:
1. Name of manufacturer
2. Brand name of food product
3. Name of food product
4. Composition
5. Net and gross weight and
6. Production and expiry dates

Arabic stickers are accepted by Customs provided they do not obscure vital information on the original labelling.

Getting your Goods to the Market

All exports to Kuwait are subject to pre-shipment inspection. A full inspection service can be provided by SGS United Kingdom Ltd. Inspection rules change frequently so exporters should check the requirements either with their customer or with the relevant pre-shipment company.

However, certain items are prohibited by the Kuwaiti Government. No goods may be imported from Israel. Alcohol, materials for making alcoholic beverages (hops, malt extracts, wine kits), arms and ammunition, unlicensed drugs and medicines, explosives, pornographic materials, politically subversive materials and pork products are all prohibited. Beef and other products from cattle from the UK and the Republic of Ireland are also prohibited. The prohibition of alcoholic beverages is strictly enforced.

Authority must be obtained from the Ministry of Health for drugs and medicines. Jewels, precious stones and metals may only be imported subject to approval by the Ministry of Commerce and Industry

Chapter 29: What are the Challenges?

Political wrangling in the country has left over $235 billion programme of megaprojects hanging in the balance, projects like: $15bn Al Zour refinery project, $2.8bn Subiya power plant project, construction projects worth $168bn, oil and gas projects $55bn, $18bn Clean Fuels Project.

Corruption and red tape

A highly bureaucratic application procedure hinders the Kuwait business climate. Foreign companies still report numerous delays in attaining approval to operate in Kuwait and FDI law of 2003 has yet to improve investment climate sufficiently.

Most companies will come across cases of bribery and corruption or what appears to be so. The Kuwait government is working hard to eradicate such activity especially in relation to government contracts. The situation is not helped by the large amount of bureaucracy and red tape that exists in Kuwait. Patience is always advised when dealing with these matters and as much as possible left to the Kuwaiti business partners to deal with.

The new Minister of commerce and Industry appointed in May 2011 has made the tackling of red tape and ease of doing business a top priority. There is also acknowledgement that corruption has to be tackled especially in the awarding of government contracts. The government has established a new capital markets authority to regulate the financial markets and the central tendering committee for government contracts continues to modify its practices in line with better international standards. This is evidenced in the move to awarding more contracts on quality of bid rather than simply lowest cost.

Terrorism Threat

There remains a general threat from terrorism. Attacks cannot be ruled out and could be indiscriminate, including in places frequented by expatriates and foreign travellers. Attacks could be directed against Western interests.

Terrorists continue to issue statements threatening to carry out attacks in the Gulf region. These include references to attacks on Western interests, including residential compounds, military, and oil, transport and aviation interests. In August 2009, Kuwaiti security forces disrupted a Kuwaiti terrorist cell and arrested six Kuwaiti nationals who were in the final stages of planning a major attack against a US military base in Kuwait. In January and February 2005, Kuwaiti security forces arrested nearly 40 suspected militants in a series of operations, some involving shooting. Bomb-making equipment and material linked with planned kidnaps were discovered. Most of those arrested have since been sentenced to death or to imprisonment. You should be aware of the global risk of indiscriminate terrorist attacks, which could be against civilian targets, including places frequented by foreigners.

Getting Paid - Terms of Payment

Exporters to Kuwait may receive payment against the value of their goods by means of any of the following:
1. Letter of credit according to which payment is made after completion of shipping formalities.
2. On CAD (Cash against Documentation) basis.
3. Direct Advance Payment.
4. Part payment, provided previous other payment were effected within the specified dates.
5. Credit sales, according to which the value of each assignment sold, shall be transferred to exporters.
6. Sales based on commission according to which the merchant sells the commodity at prevailing prices on behalf of the exporters and receive an agreed commission thereof.
7. Sales against sight drafts or promissory notes for an agreed upon period of time. Customarily this period ranges between 30 to 180 days.

How to Invest in Kuwait

The Foreign Investment Law (No. 8/2001) regulates foreign investments in Kuwait. Under the law it is intended to allow foreign investors to own up to 100% equity in Kuwaiti companies or ventures for special projects as determined by the Council of Ministers. Prior to the enactment of this law, foreign investors were subject to a ceiling of 49% (maximum) stipulated under the Law of Commerce No. 68 of 1980 and the Commercial Companies Law No. 15 of 1960. The law proposes to do away with such restrictions imposed upon foreign investors.

The Ministry of Commerce is empowered to issue licenses to foreign investors, permitting up to 100% foreign equity participation in any economic project in Kuwait. Such projects shall be exempt from the provisions of Articles 23 and 24 of the Law of Commerce as well as from the provisions of Article 68 of the Commercial Companies Law, which require at least 51% local participation. Thus, the new law proposes to overcome what was regarded by many foreign companies as a pitfall in doing business in Kuwait.

Significant steps have recently been taken to implement this law. These steps include the setting up of the Kuwait Foreign Investment Bureau (KFIB) which facilitates filing of applications and the Foreign Capital Investment Committee, headed by the Minister of Commerce and Industry to process applications for grant of licenses. Ministerial Resolution No. 23 of 2003 issued by the Minister of Commerce and Industry contains the Executive Regulations. The Regulations provide the mechanism for the implementation of the law.

CMA is an independent body that supervises trading procedures, monitors transactions and detects conflict of interests. It can resolve conflicts between investors and companies, scrutinise profit reports given by listed corporations, guarantee transparency of information, regulate take-overs and merging operations and penalise illegal activities. In short, it's the capital market's policeman and detective that maintains a fraud-free market.

Chapter 30: High Value Opportunities Available in Kuwait

UK friendship with Kuwait goes back more than 200 years and this year the UK renewed the special alliance with Kuwait. The country's commitment to increase political and economic openness will lead to a stronger, better Kuwait and to an even closer partnership between the two nations.

I believe our closer economic co-operation goes hand in hand with Kuwait's political changes. At a time of real dynamism in the Gulf, with a new generation seeking jobs and access to education, our economic partnership can be a driver of real change and a source of stability for the future.

The creation of a UK-Kuwait Trade and Investment Task Force, a new commitment to double UK trade to US$4 billion a year by 2015, and a Memorandum of Understanding (MoU) on business, trade and technical co-operation will position British business as the partner of choice for Kuwait going forward in support of their 4 Year Development Plan.

Working together to support Kuwait's development plan UK companies are well placed to secure significant business from the numerous development opportunities which the Kuwaiti Government has planned for the next few years.

Kuwait is an oil-rich economy and is the UK's 45th largest export partner. Kuwait is the UK's third largest trading partner in the Gulf Cooperation Council (GCC) countries.

The bilateral trading relationship with the United Kingdom is very healthy and still growing. UK products and services are held in very high regard by Kuwaitis. Kuwait places the same emphasis on long term relationships as other Gulf states, however some unique operational models in Kuwait, staff issues and perceived business risks are often (incorrectly) considered by UK industry to outweigh the rewards.

2011 marks a double anniversary for the State of Kuwait. Fifty years since its establishment as an Independent State, and 20 years since liberation from the Iraqi invasion. UK involvement in both events is widely appreciated and many within Kuwait see, "50/20", as an important moment in UK and Kuwaiti business relations.

Over the course of 2010 a number of landmark developments occurred which point to a maturing parliament and a realisation that the Kuwaiti Government will consider relaxing control of the private sector. Much now rests on Kuwait's ability to implement their own national development plan. The plan focuses on Kuwait's economic activity outside of the oil and finance sectors, targeting progress in many crucial infrastructure projects.

In broad terms the concerns expressed by UK companies stem from a lack of available knowledge;

concerns about corruption and procurement processes; the real need for long-term commitment; and the importance of working collaboratively with other UK, or international, partners to provide a total solution.

It is often difficult to secure accurate and up-to-date information when considering large, constantly evolving, mega-projects and the lack of (or even worse – little) knowledge can lead to misleading conclusions. However, evidence suggests this need not be a concern. UK exports of goods and services to Kuwait increased by approximately 20 per cent in the last 12 months; four out of five major development projects in Kuwait have UK professional service suppliers at their core; UK thinking, mindset and methodology are all understood widely; and, most importantly, Kuwaiti buyers are now demonstrating an increasing awareness of value-for-money over pure cost. (The financial element of a tender bid is no longer automatically considered paramount).

Chapter 31: Reform Agenda in Kuwait

The Kuwait Vision 2035 proposes reforms covers five areas:
1. Economy.
2. People.
3. Political system.
4. Cultural environment.
5. Kuwait's international positioning.

See more details below:

1. Reducing red tape: reduce requirements for starting and operating a business, improve convenience and efficiency (one-stop-shop), increase access to land and capital for start-ups and small businesses, open up international trade.

2. Improving access to land: Auction government land, engage the private sector in the development of public land and infrastructure and establish a central land authority.

3. Creating fair and equal opportunities in the market: Fight corruption and unequal treatment, develop an anti-trust law and competition commission, level the playing field for large and small enterprises, reduce government intervention in the market, lift restrictions on foreign investors and promote foreign direct investment.

4. Promoting a sound and sustainable fiscal position: Stop rapid increase in public sector employment and salaries, reduce expenditures through privatisation, reduce government spending on infrastructure and development projects (through PPP) and diversify government income.

5. Expanding and empowering the energy sector: Insulate industry from politics, become more open to international expertise, transform the electricity sector, optimise exploitation of available resources, explore the petrochemical option and build a regional energy hub.

6. Regional transport centre: Upgrade the capacity of existing infrastructure, introduce alternative management arrangements for existing infrastructure, and build a first class multimodal logistic hub that can become a gateway to the north, improve the regulatory environment for trade and develop the trade and logistics sector.

7. Developing a niche financial centre: Build a world-class financial sector, and develop a niche financial centre focused on wealth management and capital markets.

8. Changing the dynamics of the labour market: Professionalise and tighten working conditions in the public sector, prepare Kuwaitis for the private sector through training and matching skills to needs, improve working conditions in the private sector.

9. Upgrading the education system: Strengthen the teaching profession, increase the performance of students and schools, improve and adapt vocational and university education and broaden the educational choices.

10. Building a stronger healthcare system: Promote healthy lifestyles and behaviour, enhance the health infrastructure, join international prestige networks and increase the profile in international health.

11. Protecting the environment and fostering green development: Use natural resources more effectively, enhance regulation and enforcement and invest in green energy.

12. Building a cultural haven and a leisure, sport and media sanctuary: Develop an art centre, build up the creative arts and create facilities that strengthen the national image.

Furthermore, the plan calls for the issue or revision of 21 economic laws and regulations (including: privatisation, PPP, competition law, corporations law, corporate governance, income tax and securitisation) and establishing seven specialised authorities (including: stock market, high council for privatisation, transport and telecoms).

Implementation

A key feature of the 4 Year Plan is the slew of new legislations that are intended to improve efficiency, competitiveness, and governance. So far, three laws have been passed whose thrust is as follows:

1. Privatisation Law: allows the Government to privatise government owned enterprises except those involved in oil and gas production, oil refining, education and healthcare. Notwithstanding the general implication of such law, there are some features that could dilute its impact (the Government's right to retain up to 20 per cent of a privatised company with the right to veto any board decision; employees in the privatised company are allowed to keep their jobs for at least five years with salaries and benefits intact).

2. Labour Law: grants more rights to workers, though it is bound to raise employment costs substantially. In particular, the law stipulates higher end-of-service compensation, in addition to longer annual leave, official holidays and maternity leave. Furthermore, the Government would set a floor for wages every five years, while employers must provide workers with insurance coverage against work injuries or disability.

3. Capital Market Authority: the law calls for the establishment of a new authority which would regulate all financial instruments and activities to ensure competitiveness and transparency. It would also have the authority to license and supervise financial markets and regulate the process of mergers and acquisitions.

Finally, we note that the 2010/11 budget is in line with the more dynamic government plans. It calls for a 33% rise in expenditures, including a 66% rise in projects and maintenance. Spending on the latter should go from KWD 1.3 billion to 2.1 billion, a record high.

Chapter 32: Airport Expansion Opportunities in Kuwait

Within the Kuwaiti Government's 4 Year Plan is the major redesign of KIA. The development activity is split between terminal and non-terminal work.

Airport Terminal: The plans are to expand the airport terminal capacity from six million passengers per year to 20 million passengers by 2030 and turn KIA into a major regional passenger and cargo hub. The terminal development will be commissioned by the Kuwaiti Ministry of Public Works (MPW) which has recently awarded the design contract to a UK architect.

All other Development Activity: The developments include runways, infrastructure, tunnelling, fencing and cargo city will be undertaken by the end user and operator of KIA, The Directorate General of Civil Aviation (DGCA). These will include linking the new terminal to the existing terminal building via a tunnel, extending the two existing runways and the construction of a third runway.

The electrical infrastructure of the airport will also be upgraded to include a new control and communication system. A new airspace system plan will be developed, consisting of a control centre and national meteorology centre, to improve the airport's operating performance and to meet international standards.

Funding and Important Dates

The project is being funded by the Kuwait Government, through the Ministry of Public Works and the DGCA. The Government may seek a privately financed (PFI) solution for some non-terminal activities; however, the terminal building project will be fully funded by the Kuwaiti Government. All PFI activity in Kuwait is managed by the Partnerships Technical Bureau.

Design of the terminal is now well underway, and main tenders will be requested from international consultants in early 2012. Site works and enabling works are to start soon, with the construction of a 10km security fence.

Infrastructure should be completed in 2014. The terminal will initially open in 2016 with final completion of the whole airfield project by 2030.

To be successful in Kuwait requires significant commitment. Companies interested in this opportunity should consider visiting the market now and establishing a relationship with a local entity to be in a position to prepare and submit competitive tenders.

Chapter 33: Development of Kuwait City Metro

The Kuwaiti Government has agreed a complex national transport master plan that entails a complete overhaul of the country's transport infrastructure. The proposed 171km long Metro network is fundamental to these plans, and sits within the 4 Year Plan.

The network will comprise of four lines, each of which will be tendered as a separate Private Public Partnerships (PPP) contract.

Line 1 is 25.8km long and will connect Kuwait's southern metropolitan area with the centre of the city and the main university (19 stations).

Line 2 will be 21km long, connecting the main business district with the residential areas of Salmiya and Hawally and the Shuwaikh Industrial Zone (27 stations).

Line 3 will be 18.5Km long and begins at the airport and connects to the railway network and the city (15 stations).

Line 4 will be 22.7km long and begins in the new University area and residential areas, and also connects to the railway network and the city (15 stations).

The project's master plan indicates that 60km of the metro will be built underground. A UK-based consortium was successful in bidding for the eighteen months Transaction Advisor Contract for this development project. Currently, oversight of mass transport in Kuwait sits under the Ministry of Communications.

Funding and Important Dates

This project is the second PPP project announced by the Government of Kuwait since 2009, and is established through the 4 Year Plan. The whole scheme is estimated to cost US$7 billion. It is believed that The Kuwaiti Government will fund 10 per cent of the project and raise 50 per cent of the capital through an initial public offer. The balance of 40 per cent will be held by the private developer.

Chapter 34: Kuwait Hospital Development Programme

Kuwait is undertaking a programme of Health Sector reform that will focus on regulatory, financial and new-build hospital construction; taking full effect by 2020.

A National Health Authority (NHA) proposal in early 2011 transferred regulatory oversight of the Kuwaiti health sector from the Ministry of Health (MOH) to the NHA for both private and public hospitals, and also called for a stronger private healthcare sector and the establishment of a network of 15 Primary Healthcare Centres.

Ministry of Health

The MOH has subsequently allocated a budget for the renovation and expansion of nine hospital towers.

Ministry of Public Works

The MPW has a budget of £3.4 billion to construct five new private hospitals. When complete, these two initiatives will add 1,800 private beds and approximately 7,600 additional public sector beds to existing capacity.

Several other government entities have also announced hospital projects including the Kuwait Oil Company Hospital, a 350 bed general acute care facility, a Medical City plan by Kuwait Municipality, a new Police Hospital and new university teaching hospital.

Funding and Important Dates

The project is to be primarily funded by the Government of Kuwait, through the MOH and MPW as part of the 4 Year Plan.

Some projects will be developed through a PPP arrangement by the Partnerships Technical Bureau.

Tenders are expected for the eight new hospital building projects. This will commence with a 600 bed maternity hospital and will soon be followed by three 500 bed facilities in the Al-Sabah medical area in Shuwaikh, (Al-Razi, Physical Medicine, Ibn Sina hospitals). Finally, hospitals in Al Jahra (800 beds), Al Ameiri (600 beds) and Al Adan (1,000 beds) are planned.

Chapter 35: Boubyan Island Port Development

The Boubyan Island Development Project is an important initiative of the Kuwaiti Government that will include a special economic zone and a hub for transportation in the region. The Government's plan is to establish Boubyan as a major seaport which will act as a main access point for the nation of Kuwait and the surrounding area.

Boubyan, Kuwait's largest island is located in the north eastern part of the country and is separated from the mainland by the Subbiya Channel. It currently accounts for about 5 percent of the country's land area during low tide. The project is scheduled to be implemented in three phases, of which the first will be subdivided into three phases. The first part will include putting in place advanced infrastructure, treating the area's soil and creating railroad links. Part two will encompass the construction of the first section of the port while the final part will feature marine drilling, widening channels and other aspects of the construction work.

Initial infrastructure activity will include the design and construction of a 33km dual three-lane carriageway highway linking the port on the east coast of Boubyan Island with the Subiyan-Iraq Road on Kuwait mainland, and the construction of a twin line railway to run approximately parallel to the north of the highway. Both the highway and the railway are elevated at Khor Subbiya Channel crossing (approximately 1,500m wide at the crossing point). The length of the road bridge and rail bridge is about 1.5km and 9km respectively.

When completed, the port will have 60 berths stretching 1,600m into the sea. The depth at the basins of the port are projected at 16.5m, and navigation channels will be 14.5m deep.

Funding and Important Dates

The Ministry of Public Works recently announced that 48 per cent of phase one work had been completed. Various bridges will soon be completed, and the whole of phase one is scheduled for completion in 2015. No timeline has been announced for the construction of the next 12 berths to date.

Chapter 36: Kuwait Privatisation Programme

The Kuwait Financial Authority is seeking to establish itself as a serious contender to be a leading financial centre in the Gulf. In order for the Kuwait Government to deliver effectively and efficiently all that is required by the sizeable, and relatively short-term, National Development Plan, Kuwait must consider the local availability of a range of financial products.

Kuwait can easily fund all the development projects if it chooses. However, to engage better with the international private sector, and to demonstrate a commitment to knowledge sharing and transparency, the Kuwaiti Government is seeking an in-country expertise in Private-Public Partnerships (PPP) financing for future infrastructure projects.

Kuwait has passed new legislation, including a privatisation law, capital markets and labour law to help the country's small private sector to attract foreign investment.

The first PPP scheme launched was an Independent Water and Power Project and is likely to be a success as there is a proven model (and appetite) for similar schemes. The intention is to use PPP financing techniques on future national projects in the following sectors; power generation, rail, metro, hospitals and the new airport.

There are currently 32 PPP projects being developed under the management of The Partnership Technical Bureau (PTB). The pipeline for PPP projects in Kuwait is the most significant in the Middle East, with over US$25 billion worth of projects recently announced or started.

Chapter 37: Conclusion

Kuwait is a hereditary emirate, currently ruled by HH Sheikh Sabah Al-Ahmad Al-Jabir Al-Sabah. The Amir appoints a PM who appoints a further 15 Ministers to form his cabinet. There is also a 50-member elected National Assembly. Tensions between the Assembly and the Cabinet often run high and unrest within Kuwait is usually related to this – this rarely affects the UK or western interests, but the Assembly can act as a block on investment and can slow down or even stop contracts going ahead. A notable example in the past few years was a major contract with Dow Chemical's which was granted by the government, but then blocked by the Assembly.

Kuwait's Ruling Family and democratic foundations remains firmly rooted, former Prime Minister Sheikh Nasser Al Mohammad Al Sabah and his Cabinet resigned on November 28 against the backdrop of corruption allegations and criticism of perceived governmental mismanagement. Following his appointment of a new Prime Minister (and former Defence Minister) Sheikh Jaber Sheikh Jaber will ran a care-taker administration.

Kuwait is the world's sixth largest oil exporter, sits on 10% of known oil reserves and nominal GDP rose 16.9% last year. But there are issues that need addressing. The Finance Minister has warned that the oil-dominated economy (90% of revenue comes from the state-owned oil industry) is on an unsustainable trajectory. The budget has tripled since 2004, although it remains in credit, for now. The biggest concern is the growth of the non-productive public sector which accounts for 85% of Government expenditure.

The Government is addressing the problem through the public/private funded £90+ billion Development Plan. This aims to privatise loss making state enterprises and diversify away from oil by creating a vibrant private sector.

Kuwait will enjoy a further large budget surplus in 2011/12, but its economic outlook may falter if oil prices threaten to fall. Spending on the £93billion Development Plan has stalled as domestic political wrangling threatens to delay further economic development. UK companies remain well positioned to gain very significant work under Kuwait's Development Plan, when implementation eventually resumes.

Private sector growth is a key component of Kuwait's four-year £93 billion Development Plan. It aims to diversify Kuwait's economy, with investors expected to meet almost half the cost. However, while Government spending has increased significantly so far this financial year, it has done so almost entirely on the beck of increased public sector wages and allowances. Spending on the implementation of the Development Plan has stalled, especially private sector involvement. The growing public-sector raises serious questions about fiscal sustainability, as large public-sector wage increases and generous benefits continue to undermine incentives for Kuwaitis to move into the private sector. HSBC estimates that Kuwait will be the only member of the GCC to experience a slowdown in private-sector credit growth in 2012; a concern shared by the Governor of the Central Bank, who warned recently that "without urgent and rapid capital spending on various state projects, there will be no growth and, without providing good investment opportunities to the private sector to expand its local financial activities, the future outlook will be limited".

Will things improve?

The growing seriousness of the problem means that an increasing number of senior politicians recognise the need to begin to educate the wider population about the requirement for reform, with a clear focus on diversification away from oil and the establishment of a private sector through rapid implementation of the Development Plan. These voices are likely to become louder in years to come

Kuwait is coming out of the shadow of the global economic crisis and its own recent past. In relative terms, Kuwait was well protected from the Global economic crisis. The conservative investment policies it had pursued since the 1990 invasion protected it from big losses, as did the Sovereign Wealth Funds diverse investment portfolio. Against that, Kuwait's economic development since liberation in 1991 has lagged behind others in the region. Despite the government's laudable aim of improving economic efficiency and guaranteeing social equality, the state's dominant economic role has led to a bloated and inefficient bureaucracy, which has impeded the growth of the private sector and contributed to a relatively weak business environment, numerous subsidies and an overall dependence of economic activity on oil revenues and government expenditures. But recent movement politically, as the parliament and government begin to work together for the first time in over a decade, is having a knock on effect on the economy. Kuwait now seeks to regain its position as a regional financial, business and transport centre within the GCC.

On February 2, 2010 the National Assembly approved the Four Year Development plan (2010-2014), the government's first plan since 1986 and part of the wider vision of Kuwait 2035. The 2035 vision states that Kuwait must be transformed into a regional financial and business hub, attracting investment. The economy should be led by the private sector supported by the government and it's institutions to ensure balanced development with appropriate infrastructure, legislation and a positive business atmosphere. The four year plan costing thirty billion Kuwaiti Dinars (£93 billion) is being co-ordinated by the Amir's nephew Sheikh Ahmad Al Fahad Al Sabah the Deputy Premier for Economic Affairs, State Minister for Housing and Development. It aims to diversify the economy away from oil, attract more Foreign Direct investment into the country, and boost the participation of the private sector in government projects.

The plan has five key objectives:

Increase total national production and upgrade living standards of citizens through increasing growth in non-oil sectors (diversification into the financial, trade, services, and petro-chemical sectors). Financial institutions should increase competitiveness (both in Islamic and conventional financing).

The private sector should be a catalyst for development, gradually reducing the role of the public sector. Simplified investment procedures for the private sector, the completion of basic infrastructure projects and integration between the public and private sectors should be achieved.

Support for human and societal development through developing education, training, scientific research, health services, environment and sustainable systems, encouraging female empowerment, youth projects, housing, culture, press and religious affairs.

Developing housing policies to support a growing population (Kuwaitis and non- Kuwaitis).

Effective governance through transparency in society and the economy. This should involve restructuring of the governmental sector institutionally, organisationally and electronically in order to improve public and business services. Planning, IT and statistical activities should be activated.

Part 4: CEO Guide to Doing Business in Bahrain

Chapter 38: Introduction

Bahrain is a small island with a population of just over 1 million people. Bahrain's total area covers 770 sq km; it is the smallest of the six Gulf Cooperation Council (GCC) member states and consists of 33 islands.

Strategically located with a 25 km causeway connection to Saudi Arabia and the rest of the GCC, Bahrain is seen as a gateway to the Gulf, a market of over 100 million people. A 40 km causeway to Qatar is scheduled for completion by 2015. In addition to its geographical location, the discovery of oil in 1932 laid the foundation from which Bahrain is transforming into a modern diversified economy.

Strengths of the market
1. The operational costs are amongst the most competitive in the region.
2. Bahrain is strategically located in the Northern Gulf with good communication links into Saudi Arabia and beyond.
3. Bahrain is recognised as having strong and effective regulation in Financial Services and other sectors.
4. Bahrain has the most educated and skilled workforce in the Gulf.
5. Bahrain was ranked the most open and liberal business environment in the Middle East, and 13th in the world (Source: Index of Economic Freedom, 2010)

6. Bahrain has the longest track record in business in the region.
7. Bahrain has ranked highly for quality of life for expatriates.

Opportunities in Bahrain

A recognised global centre for Islamic Finance in particular, Financial Services contributes approximately 25% of GDP. Manufacturing contributes 16% and the oil and gas industry 13% of GDP. Bahrain has embarked on a programme of privatisation, which includes telecommunications, electricity and water, the ports and airport services.

The principal sectors where businesses will find opportunity areas are:
1. Financial & Professional Services
2. Education & Skills
3. Infrastructure
4. Healthcare
5. Business services
6. Downstream Manufacturing (from metals, petrochemicals)

Bahrain is one of the UK's smallest export markets in the Gulf countries and is a major trading hub and financial centre in the Middle East. Trade in goods between the UK and Bahrain remains strong despite a slight decline in UK export figures in 2010, compared to the same period in 2009.

Chapter 39: Bahrain Economic and Political Overview

Although Bahrain's economy is relatively small and under the shadow of the economic power houses of Saudi Arabia and the UAE, it has the most liberalised economy of The GCC. They began a programme of education, labour market and economic reforms from (circa) 2006 to enhance its competitiveness in the modern global economy. It's favourable tax regime (the most liberal in the Gulf), low cost base, proximity to Kingdom of Saudi Arabia, reputation for transparent regulations and good quality of life, have helped it to compete for international trade and investment.

Like most Gulf economies, Bahrain relies heavily on oil and gas, but its resources are quickly running dry forcing the need to diversify the economy into other sectors, and to look at developing non-oil government revenue, including (e.g.) value-added tax. The Bahrainis have successfully built up the tourism (including annual F1 Grand Prix), metals (particularly aluminium), transport and financial sectors.

In Bahrain, petroleum production and processing account for about 60% of export receipts, 70% of government revenues, and circa 12% of GDP, exclusive of allied industries. Aluminium is Bahrain's second major export after oil and gas. With its highly developed communication and transport facilities, Bahrain is home to numerous multinational firms with business in the Gulf region. Financial and insurance services contribute over 25% of GDP. The latest data shows that Bahrain's real GDP grew by 4.3% year-on-year in the third quarter of 2010 Real growth reached 4.1% for the year as a whole.

Population

Bahrain's population is estimated at just over 1million people; approx: 50% are expatriates workers from India, Pakistan, Bangladesh and Philippines plus western expatriates. Bahrain's business sector is supported by the most productive, highly-skilled bilingual national work force in the GCC (approx: 72% of the financial services work force is Bahraini).

Political Overview

The UK Bahrain relationship is traditionally close. There are strong historical ties, and many of the leading Bahrainis have studied in the UK and / or have property and interests there. The ruling family has a close relationship with the UK Royal Family, as well as close ties to the military, particularly Sandhurst. British advisers were instrumental in the establishment of the Bahraini system of government, and many British nationals currently work, independently, within Bahraini Ministries.

HM King Hamad bin Isa Al-Khalifa succeeded his father (Shaikh Isa bin Sulman Al-Khalifa) as Ruler in 1999 on the latter's death, and began to transform Bahrain into a constitutional monarchy. HM King Hamad pardoned political prisoners and detainees in

2001, including those previously exiled from Bahrain. He also abolished the State Security Law and State Security Court, which were much criticised by opposition groups for suppressing freedom. After referendums and consultation, HM King Hamad presented Bahrain's new Constitution on 14 February 2002, which set out plans for a bi-cameral Parliament (the National Assembly) and transformed Bahrain into a Kingdom. The Parliament comprises two Houses - the Shura (Consultative, Upper House) and the Nuwab (Lower House, Council of Representatives). Both Councils consist of 40 members, the Shura appointed by the King, and the Nuwab elected by the public. Members of both Councils serve four-year terms. Sessions of the Shura and Nuwab are open to the public, unless the government requests a closed session.

In February and March 2011 protestors took to the streets in increasingly large numbers calling for reform. These protests descended into violence, prompting a security crackdown, backed by GCC forces. HM the King declared a State of National Safety on 16 March 2011, and then lifted it on 1st June 2011 once security had been re-established. However, deep underlying sectarian tensions remain, and the process towards achieving reconciliation and genuine stability may take some time.

Chapter 40: Getting to Bahrain and Advice About Your Stay

Bahrain is accessible by air, sea and road. Driving is permitted on a valid UK licence and will automatically be transferred after relevant documents have been issued (work/residence permit, CPR cards)

By road

Connection with neighbouring countries, 25 km King Fahad Causeway linking Bahrain and Saudi Arabia provides easy access to the Saudi market. A 40 km causeway to Qatar is also planned.

By sea

The official inauguration of the Kingdom's new state-of-the-art Khalifa Bin Salman port took place 11 November 2009. More than USD 600 million total investment volume.

By air

Bahrain International Airport is a key hub airport in the region, providing a gateway to the Northern Gulf. The airport is a major hub for both Gulf Air and Bahrain Air operating 460 and 136 flights respectively. There are 39 other international airlines including British Airways, Cathay Pacific, KLM and Lufthansa operate a total of 460 services per week to a total of 60 destinations.

Visas for Bahrain

Visas are required by all visitors to Bahrain except passport holders of the GCC States. All other visitors require one of the following visas:

Visiting and Tourist Visas

Two Weeks Tourist Visas: Tourist visas are issued for stays of two weeks to citizens of the European Union (EU), Australia, Canada, Hong Kong, Japan, New Zealand and the USA. Applicants must possess valid, up-to-date passports and a return or onward ticket. A visa fee of BD5 ($12) is applied and can be obtained at entry at the Bahrain International Airport. Tourist visas don't allow visitors to engage in any employment.

72 hour/7 day Visas Can be obtained on arrival at the Bahrain International Airport or at the King Fahad Causeway. In addition to a passport, the passenger must have a confirmed return/onward journey ticket for the visa application to be processed.

Health Insurance

It is recommended to take out full medical insurance when visiting Bahrain as there no reciprocal healthcare agreements between Bahrain and UK. All visitors intending to travel to Bahrain are strongly advised to check the current health regulations with their travel agents or Bahrain Embassy.

Medical Services

Medical services in Bahrain are of high quality, with good general hospitals and modern health centres in smaller communities. American Mission Hospital, Awali Hospital, International Hospital of Bahrain and Bahrain Specialist Hospital to name a few who all offer private walk-in consultations.

Chapter 41: Bahrain Market Entry and Start up Considerations

The commercial laws and legal system are under constant review to ensure that they are consistent with international standards. The Kingdom of Bahrain permits 100% foreign ownership of businesses. Companies operating in Bahrain are expected to follow the international accounting standards and are encouraged to pursue good corporate governance.

Your first port of call in setting up a business/office in Bahrain would be a visit to the Bahrain Investor's Centre which is a vital part of the Ministry of Commerce. The One Stop Shop "Bahrain Investor's Centre" has been established to facilitate the setting up of business in Bahrain through a seamless process. They are here to facilitate the entire process, from the submission of the initial application to the commencement of business. The back office will guide you to relevant external entities such as the Ministry of Labour and Ministry of Interior who will be able to advice on requirements for residency for expatriates.

The Bahrain International Investment Park (BIIP) is a new, quality, 247 Hectare Business Park developed in Bahrain by the Ministry of Industry and Commerce. The Park is situated in a superb location with excellent connectivity and access. Bahrain

International Airport and the new Shaikh Khalifa Port in Hidd are both just 5 minutes away by road. The BIIP also enjoys direct motorway access to Saudi Arabia, via the 25km Saudi-Bahrain Causeway, only 20 minutes away and by 2010 will enjoy the same connectivity to Qatar.

The BIIP is designed to attract export oriented, local and global companies with high value-added projects that will contribute to creating quality local employment in a world class physical environment. www.biip.com.bh

Bahrain Investment Wharf (BIW) provides the vital means for your investments by setting all essential details allowing you to enhance your productivity and maximizing profitability. BIW is ideally suited for various sectors, which may include: Light industries, including warehousing and logistics, Medium industries Business centres, Commercial and residential facilities. www.bahiw.com

The Khalifa Bin Salman Port is considered to be one of the most important and advanced ports in the Gulf region. It is also one of the most vital infrastructure projects that aims to enhance various economic sectors, particularly the commercial, industrial, and investment sectors in the Kingdom. The port will also help promote Bahrain's strategic location as a regional and international commercial and financial hub. The Khalifa bin Salman Port occupies an area of 110 hectares of reclaimed land and is located on the north-east of the Kingdom of Bahrain, only 13 kilometres away from Bahrain International Airport, and it is also linked to the road leading to the King Fahad Causeway. The port provides sea freight, shipping, and logistic services in accordance to the highest international specifications and standards in the industry. Website of the General Organisation of Sea Ports (GOP) www.gop.org.bh

The Bahrain Logistics Zone

Based at the heart of the Gulf, in the Kingdom of Bahrain, the Zone offers logistics organisations an unbeatable location for providing services to the growing economies of the Gulf region.

As a boutique logistics area, it is dedicated to value-adding activities, catering for companies engaged in a variety of intensive logistics activities.

It offers its tenants a range of services to match the requirements of modern logistics organisations, from streamlined customs processes to on-site company registration and visa application. The Bahrain Logistics Zone is owned and operated by the General Organisation of Sea Ports, Bahrain. www.bahrainlogisticszone.com

The Bahrain Financial Harbour (BFH) is a fully integrated US $3billion master-planned development. It is creating a complete financial city, a self contained community and reinforcing Bahrain's unique position as the financial capital of the Middle East. A first of its kind development in the region, BFH is a highly focused, committed and advanced financial environment spread over 380,000 square metres of prime seafront property in the centre of Manama, Kingdom of Bahrain. Furthermore, it comprises 10 projects that distinctively combine business, leisure and residential components under one canopy. Phase I of the project 'The Financial Centre' which includes the Harbour Towers - Bahrain's tallest towers and the Harbour Mall. The Financial Centre is operational and open for business. www.bfharbour.com

Chapter 42: Customs and Regulations in Bahrain

Goods imported into the country are subject to the customs taxes "duties" specified in the customs tariff, and the other applicable fees, excluding those exempted under the provisions of this regulation law or under the Unified Economic Agreement of the GCC Arab states or any other international agreement within the framework of the Council. The duty rate of the customs tariff shall be either ad Valorem (percentage of the value of goods) or specific (an amount levied on each unit of the goods), or both.

Customs duties are usually 5% for imported goods, with the exception for alcohol (125%) and tobacco (100%) Numerous food and medical items are entirely exempt from customs duty as well as goods for re-export, capital goods, and raw materials for manufacturing imports required for development projects.

The commercial laws and legal system are under constant review to ensure that they are consistent with international standards. Companies operating in Bahrain are expected to follow the international accounting standards and are encouraged to pursue good corporate governance. Bahrain has a zero-tolerance policy for money laundering and enforces best-practice international standards of intellectual property, labour and environment protection.

Currency and Taxation

1. There are no Exchange Controls on the movement of monies.
2. Bahrain's currency is the Bahrain Dinar (BD), which is pegged to the US Dollar.
3. Bahrain has the lowest corporate and personal taxes in the GCC with:
   a. No capital gains tax and no withholding tax.
   b. No personal income tax.
   c. No tax on capital gains.
   d. No withholding tax.
   e. No restriction on repatriation of capital, profits or dividends.
   f. Few indirect taxes (e.g. 10% municipal tax on rents).

Responding to Tenders

The Tender Board is a fully independent body, established by a Royal Decree on 7 January 2003, with a clear agenda to set up a strict regulatory mechanism that would ensure fairness and equal opportunity for all.

The Tender Board aims to protect public funds and prevent the undue influence of personal interests on tender formalities; achieve maximum levels of economic efficiency in purchasing activities at competitive and fair prices; encourage integrity, competitiveness, fair treatment and equal opportunity to all contractors and suppliers; and finally, to achieve total transparency in all aspects of purchasing procedures by the Government.

The Tender Board's achievements over the past three years have earned it a reputation for transparency, integrity, fairness, competitiveness and equal opportunity. This has undoubtedly played a major role in boosting investors' confidence in the nation's economy, and enhancing the prestigious status of the Kingdom of Bahrain, both regionally and internationally. www.tenderboard.gov.bh

Recruiting and Retaining Staff

Bahrain's business sector is supported by the most productive, highly-skilled bilingual national work force in the GCC (approximately 72% of the financial services workforce are Bahraini) Bahrain has an advanced education system, which continues to improve. Bahrain's government has introduced education reforms that will continue to improve education and skills in line with the requirements of the private sector, adopting best practice from some of the world's most successful educational models. The government of Bahrain realizes that highly skilled and highly specialized positions require appropriately qualified individuals to fill them. This is why Bahraini businesses have the opportunity to choose between the local work force or hire foreign specialists for these positions.

Documentation

Current requirements to live and work in Bahrain Anyone wishing to live and legally work in Bahrain will need to apply for the following visas and permits:

1. Work Visa - issued by Labour Market Regulatory Authority (LMRA) www.lmra.bh
2. Residency Permit - issued by General Department for Nationality & Passport Residence www.gdnpr.gov.bh
3. CPR Card (Identification Card) - issued by Central Informatics Organisation. www.cio.gov.bh

Employers are advised to arrange and process necessary documents to the Labour Market Regulatory Authority (LMRA) prior to the arrival of their employees and dependents.

Labelling and Packaging Regulations

According to Bahraini regulations, all labelling must be in Arabic or Arabic/English. Stickers are not accepted as adequate labelling.

Food labels must include:
1. Product and brand names.
2. Production and expiry dates.
3. Country of origin.
4. Name of manufacturer.
5. Net weight (metric units)
6. List of ingredients and additives in descending order of importance.

Getting Your Goods to the Market

For the clearance of imported goods and commodities, the importers should complete the customs declaration and to present it together with other required documents to the customs gateway concerned so that the customs clearance procedures will begin. www.bahraincustoms.gov.bh

Mina Salman Port is currently the main port of Bahrain for General Cargo and Containers. This port can handle dry cargoes (conventional and containers) with an average annual volume of 2.5 million tonnes. Mina Salman Port was open in 1962, since that time the Government made determined efforts to modernize and improve the efficiency and capacity of Mina Salman. The port comprises 15 berths, two of them are container berths, and the rest are conventional cargo berths which can accommodate different sizes of ships with different draughts varying between 5.5 to 10 meters. A small Ro-Ro ramp is available for vessels up to 15meters wide.

The Khalifa Bin Salman Port and its adjacent Industrial Area is located towards the North Eastern extremity of Bahrain. 5kms from the Bahrain International Airport, this project is a part of an extensive development program of more than 800 hectares of land. This new facility will ensure an excellent level of services to the shipping lines and support Bahrain's industrial growth.

Standards and Technical Regulation

The Ministry of Industry and Commerce, in particular as the main organ of Government responsible for the registration and supervision of businesses in Bahrain, perceives its role as providing value added services to its customers in the form of enhanced information and business processes.

The Ministry of Industry and Commerce is responsible for a diverse range of activities which make up the commercial environment in Bahrain, including inter alia the registration of all forms of commercial business, commercial agencies, industrial property, standards and metrology, foreign trade as well as a number of other related activities. In general the Ministry's aim is to ensure the maintenance of an open, transparent and market driven commercial environment so as to develop Bahrain's economic competitiveness, and to encourage inward investment, at the same time promoting employment for the local population. Website: www.moic.gov.bh

Chapter 43: Bahrain Business Etiquette, Language and Culture

Whilst Bahrain is the most liberal of Arab states and Bahrainis are well known for their hospitable nature, it may be the winning advantage to understand the basics of Arab etiquette.

Be prepared to wait or even to have a meeting postponed or cancelled at the last minute. Arabs hold a very different perception of time to that of a westerner and in addition, a more senior person may have requested his presence at short notice, which he will be obligated to attend.

Do's and Don'ts

1. Shaking hands – only use your right hand, and do not shake hands with a woman unless she specifically offers it. In addition, women should not attempt to shake an Arab man's hand unless he extends his hand to her first.

2. Greetings – although Arabs will almost certainly greet you in English, you may gain enormous kudos if you are able to speak a little Arabic. The most common greeting is As-salaam alaykum (literally peace be on you) with the reply of Wa alaykum as-salaam (And on you be peace).

3. It is customary to initially start the meeting with enquiries regarding each other's health,

no matter how frequently you meet someone or talk on the phone. This is followed with enquiries about the family which should be restricted to the collective family and children and not after an Arab's wife, unless you know the family very well.

4. Tafaddal (be so good as to. take a seat). When you enter an office of an Arab for a business meeting do not be surprised if it is full of other visitors; senior Arabs will routinely receive large numbers of visitors a day. Once you have presented your business card, a seat will then be indicated to you with the word tafaddal. If the room is crowded it will usually be next to the host. When someone else arrives you should stand up, shake hands with the newcomer and be prepared to vacate your seat for him, take your lead from your host.

5. The Sole of the Foot – avoid presenting the sole of your foot directly at another person. It is traditionally considered unclean and can be used to intentionally insult a person. It is advisable to sit with both feet on the floor. Do not cross your legs unless your host does so and even then avoid presenting your sole directly at him.

6. Refreshments. If your host abides by the traditional custom, the initial greetings will be followed by a period of silence until a servant enters with refreshments, which you should always accept. Only ever use your right hand

even if you are left-handed. It is usual to drink two or three cups, but no more than your host. When you have had enough, give your little coffee cup a quick twist or shake when handing it back, if you merely offer it to the server he will refill it.

7. Broaching the subject of your visit normally occurs after refreshments have been served; your host will normally give you an indication.

8. Silence – do not worry about pauses in conversation, silences are not embarrassing to an Arab and shows gravitas.

9. Never expect a topic to be raised, discussed and a decision is not usually taken on your first visit; an Arab will wish to get to know you but also consider the matter before giving you a decision.

10. Interruptions – because of the open-door policy of the Arab culture anyone may call on your host at any time and will receive the same courteous welcome as yourself.

11. Business in Bahrain is based on a mood of trust in which early/frequent requests for payment can seem premature to many Bahrainis. This reiterates the need to build good business relationships, which will take time.

12. Taking your leave – initial visits are usually short so do not attempt to achieve all results

185

at the first meeting and overstaying your welcome could jeopardise your chances later on. The phrase for goodbye is

a.   Greeting; Maa as-salaama (With the peace (on you))
b.   Reply: Maa as-salaama or Allah yisullmak (God protect you)

Language

The official language of Bahrain is Arabic; however English is widely spoken as well. It is used in business and is a compulsory second language in schools. In addition, all signs are in both English and Arabic. Given the large size of expatriate population in Bahrain, a variety of other languages are also widely spoken, such as Urdu, Hindi and Farsi.

Meetings and Presentations

Senior people in the Bahrain companies are generally very accessible to visitors, particularly foreign business visitors. However, local business people do not like making appointments a long time in advance. It is always worth calling them prior to your visit to check they will be in the country at a particular time. Be prepared to wait as meetings can take time to fix, and arrangements may be changed at the last minute, or you may be kept waiting because previous engagements have been altered or have overrun.

A personal relationship with your customer is the foundation of successful business in the region, and a successful business development strategy for Bahrain is one that takes a long-term view. Many local companies will not enter into a business relationship until personal trust has been established, and this can take several meetings and visits to build. Do not expect to win orders on your first visit (although this does happen on rare occasions) and be prepared to travel to the region several times to cultivate potential customers. Once you have built these relationships take care to maintain them, through regular visits to the market.

Chapter 44: Business Overview in Bahrain

Bahrain is an open business friendly country; there are no major challenges to doing business in Bahrain. Bankruptcy insolvency laws provide a better environment for creditors in Bahrain than in other parts of the MENA Region.

Getting Paid - Terms of Payment

The preferred method of payment for exports is a Letter of Credit (LC). Other means may be used with suitable safeguards. Difficulty can be minimised through sound credit management, clear agreement with the customer on payment terms and procedures and correct documentation.

How to Invest in the Kingdom of Bahrain

The Economic Development Board (EDB) is a dynamic Government agency with an overall responsibility for formulating and overseeing the economic development strategy of the Kingdom of Bahrain and for creating the right climate to attract direct investment into the Kingdom. The EDB aims to create the optimum business environment for Bahrain, to ensure the country attracts investment from abroad, as well as encouraging the strong development of home-grown companies.

The EDB offers an investor facilitation service to first-time investors who are interested in setting-up investment projects in Bahrain. This service includes acting as the investor's first point of contact in the Kingdom, providing information and guidance regarding the relevant procedures and incentives, and helping them form a network of contacts in Bahrain. In addition, the EDB co-ordinates with all relevant government bodies to help resolve difficulties that an investor may encounter during the approval and registration process. The EDB supports and monitors initiatives that improve the economic and business environment in Bahrain.

Financial Assistance

A wide range of credit and commercial loan arrangements are available to local and international investors through the various Islamic and conventional banks and financial institutions in Bahrain. Financing is also available through the Bahrain Development Bank and the Bahrain Stock Exchange. The Bahrain Development Bank (BDB) provides a variety of financial services that are tailored to meet the needs of small and medium businesses in Bahrain and promote the development of small and medium-sized projects in both the industrial and service sectors.

The state-owned bank assists aspiring and existing investors to help initiate new projects and businesses. It provides loans at highly competitive interest rates, in addition to business advisory/counselling, and training through the Entrepreneurship

Development and Enterprise Creation Programme.

Foreign-owned companies are eligible for partial financing, provided they meet certain criteria such as providing training and employment to a significant number of Bahrainis.

Chapter 45: Bahrain: What are the Challenges?

Security has been established in Bahrain following widespread demonstrations and some violence through the first half of 2011. But the underlying political situation remains tense and uncertain, and outbreaks of violence continue in some villages.

The government has announced plans to achieve reform and reconciliation, including establishing the Bahrain Independent Commission of Inquiry to look into the events of February, March and subsequently. The Independent Commission will present its findings on 23 November 2011. The report and implementation of its recommendations are likely to be critical to establishing long-term underlying stability in Bahrain.

The government is a Monarchy, with His Majesty King Hamad bin Isa Al Khalifa as Head of State. There is also a bi-cameral Parliament (the National Assembly), comprising of the Shura Council (appointed by the King) and the Nuwab (elected by universal suffrage). Both Councils consist of 40 members and the last full elections to the Nuwab were in October 2010, with by-elections for 18 seats subsequently vacated held in October 2011.

In 2010 The World Bank's Doing Business project ranked Bahrain 20 in the overall "Ease of Doing Business" table (out of 183 economies)

Bribery and Corruption

Bahrain has one of the most transparent and well regulated economies in the Middle East. According to the NGO Transparency International Corruption Perception Index (CPI), in 2009 Bahrain ranked in 46th place globally. Bahrain had the 4th lowest perceived level of corruption in the Middle East and North Africa Region in 2008. As with all business dealings though, we recommend you take legal advice from a local lawyer when necessary.

Terrorism Threat

The Centre for the Protection of National Infrastructure also provides protective security advice to businesses

The general threat from terrorism in Bahrain remains. Terrorists continue to issue statements threatening to carry out attacks in the Gulf region. These include references to attacks on Western interests, including residential compounds, military, oil transport and aviation interests.

Chapter 46: Intellectual Property Rights

Intellectual property is dealt with by the Industrial Property Directorate in the Ministry of Industry and Commerce. Industrial Property legislation was issued in 1955 for patents, design and trademarks through the Industrial Property office. The Industrial Property Office was considered to be one of the oldest IP offices in the Gulf, and it gained a good international reputation.

The Ministry of Industry and Commerce is responsible for a diverse range of activities which make up the commercial environment in Bahrain, including the registration of all forms of commercial business, commercial agencies, industrial property, standards and metrology, foreign trade as well as a number of other related activities. In general the Ministry's aim is to ensure the maintenance of an open, transparent and market driven commercial environment.

The Ministry of Industry & Commerce is responsible for a diverse range of activities which make up the commercial environment in Bahrain, including the registration of all forms of commercial business, commercial agencies, industrial property, standards & metrology, foreign trade as well as a number of other related activities. In general the Ministry's aim is to ensure the maintenance of an open, transparent and market driven commercial environment

The U.S. - Bahrain FTA commits Bahrain to enforce world -class protection of intellectual property rights. Bahrain signed the Berne Convention for the Protection of Literary and Artistic Works and the Paris Convention for the Protection of Industrial Property in 1996. Bahrain has joined the Patent Cooperation Treaty, Madrid Agreement, the World Intellectual Property Organisation (WIPO) Copyright Treaty, WIPO Performances and Phonograms Treaty, the Rome Convention, the International Convention for the Protection of New Varieties of Plants and the Patent Law Treaty.

Following the FTA, Bahrain ratified the Budapest Treaty, the Trademark Law, and the Convention Relating to the Distribution of Programme-Carrying Signals Transmitted by Satellite in 2006. At the same time, the government also passed the following WIPO-compliant laws regarding:
1. Trade secrets.
2. Copyright and related rights.
3. Designs of integrated circuits.
4. Geographic indicators.
5. Individual drawings and designs.
6. Patents and utility models.
7. Plant varieties T.

The government's copyright enforcement campaign began in late 1997 and was based on inspections, closures, and improved public awareness. The campaign targeted the video, audio and software businesses, with impressive results. Bahrain has been aggressive in combating video and audio piracy.

There are no technology transfer requirements that force firms to share or divulge technology through compulsory licensing to a domestic partner. Firms are not obliged to undertake research and development activities in Bahrain.

Chapter 47: Conclusion

In order to fully comprehend the culture of Bahrain, it is important to understand the influence of religion on society. Islam is practised by the majority of Bahrainis, who mainly belong to the Shi'a branch of Islam. Known as the most progressive Islamic country in the Middle East, Bahraini law is based on a combination of Islamic law and English common law.

Islam governs many aspects of a Muslim's life, from holidays to the food they eat to how they dress and do business. Generosity, modesty and respect for others are key concepts which are present in both social and professional spheres of life. However, reforms and more Western approaches have been introduced in Bahrain.

Bahrainis are known for their hospitality in both social and professional contexts. They welcome guests warmly and with a variety of traditions and rituals, the most important of which is the serving of coffee or tea which is provided at even the shortest meeting. Greetings are very important in Bahrain and Bahrainis take their time, often holding the hand of their counterpart throughout the entire duration of the greeting process.

Bahraini hospitality is part of their desire to establish trust and build relationships with people before doing business. Foreigners should therefore show their gratitude for this generosity and spend time getting acquainted with their Bahraini business counterparts.

Bahraini culture places a high importance on family. Extended family ties are paramount and Bahrainis are known to fiercely defend their family's honour. Loyalty to the family comes before anything else, even in a business context where it is not uncommon to have several members of one family working for the same company.

Communication in the Middle East tends to be relatively indirect and relies heavily on nonverbal cues and figurative forms of speech, where information is not explicitly stated. Respecting an individual's honour and saving face are key drivers in the indirect communication style that is prevalent throughout the Middle East. Directly refusing a proposal, for example, may be interpreted as impolite. Therefore, when conducting business discussions with your Middle Eastern colleagues you should avoid responding with a direct "no", and be prepared to interpret seemingly indefinite comments and gestures. It is also impolite to directly criticise a Middle Eastern counterpart as it brings shame to the person's honour.

Bahrain has opened itself relatively early to the world and has since developed into a modern, flourishing country. Its natural resources, excellent infrastructure and low taxation make the country to an ideal investment location. Bahrain was the first country in the Arabian Gulf in which oil was discovered. Today, Bahrain's efforts to modernise and open its borders combined with its attractive economy is increasingly drawing interest from foreign investors. Investing or doing business in Bahrain successfully requires an in-depth understanding of Bahrain's unique business culture and etiquette.

Good Luck!

Part 5: CEO Guide to Doing Business in Qatar

Chapter 48: Introduction

Are you a UK company interested in exporting to Qatar?

The main objective of this book is to provide you with basic knowledge about doing business in Qatar.

The State of Qatar is located on the east coast of the Arabian Peninsula, bordered by Saudi Arabia to the south. It has an area of 11,435 sq km (roughly half the size of Wales). Its capital city is Doha and other major towns are Ras Laffan, Al Khor, Mesaieed, Dukhan and Al Rayyan. Qatar's population is 1.7 million according to the national census in 2010 (an increase of 128% since the last official census of 2004, when the population stood at 740,000). 76% of the population is male and 24% is female. Unofficial estimates are that round 80% of the population is comprised of expatriates (mostly other Arab, South and East Asian, European and American). Approximately 20% of the population are Qatari nationals. Qatar is an Arab nation with Islam as the official religion. Arabic is the official language but English is also widely used.

The main source of Qatar's wealth is its vast reserves of oil and natural gas (it has the world's 3rd largest natural gas reserves) which have made it one of the richest countries in the world. Prudent management of these reserves has produced substantial fiscal surpluses (estimated at $16bn, or 3.4% of GDP, for 2010-11) that are being used to fund a diversification and development programme of investment in energy related industries, health, education and infrastructure in particular.

British exports to Qatar have more than doubled in the last few years. Qatar is a significant investor in the UK and has a growing portfolio of UK property. The UK imports more by value from Qatar than any other country in the region. With one of the highest rates of GDP per capita in the world and a stable government and economy there is real potential for UK companies to bring their products and services to Qatar. UK goods and services generally enjoy a strong reputation. The Qatar National Vision 2030, published in 2008 sets out Qatar's strategy and development and priorities.

Qatar's Emir, His Highness Sheikh Hamad bin Khalifa Al-Thani, has ruled since 1995 when he took over power from his father. His son, His Highness Sheikh Tamim bin Hamad Al-Thani, was appointed the Heir Apparent in 2003. His Excellency Sheikh Hamad bin Jassim bin Jabor Al-Thani was appointed Prime Minister in 2007, as well as continuing in his existing role as Minister of Foreign Affairs. The Deputy Prime Minister and Chief of the Emiri Diwan is His Excellency Abdullah bin Hamad Al-Attiyah. The Emir's consort, Skeikha Mozah bint Nasser Al-Missned, is a leading figure in the country.

Qatar's first elections to the Central Municipal Council took place in 1999, with subsequent elections in 2003 and 2007. In 2003 97% of Qataris supported a new constitution in a national referendum. The new constitution came into force in June 2005 and provides for elections to a 45 member Legislative Council (Majils al-Shura). Two thirds of the council will be elected, with the Emir appointing the remainder. The constitution also contains provisions for the establishment of an independent judiciary, equal rights for men and women and freedom of expression for the press, freedom of assembly and freedom of worship. Some elements of the constitution have yet to be fully implemented.

Qatar is a member of several international organizations, including the League of Arab States, the Gulf Cooperation Council (GCC), the Organisation of the Islamic Conference (OIC), the Organisation of the Petroleum Exporting Countries (OPEC) and the United Nations (where it was a member of the Security Council from 2005 to 2007).

The Qatari government owns Al Jazeera, the satellite television station, which broadcasts in both Arabic and English from Qatar. In 2006 Al Jazeera launched an English language TV channel with one of its four broadcast centres in London.

The exploitation of significant gas reserves has made Qatar a key strategic energy supplier to the world's major economies. Oil and gas (which account for around 50% of Qatar's GDP) are the major driving forces of Qatar's economy one of the world's fastest-growing. Safeguarding and maximizing oil and gas revenue therefore remains central to Qatar's economic development and to its desire to diversify its economy. During the last few years Qatar has experienced the highest average growth rate in the Gulf Cooperation Council (GCC) and in 2010 had the highest growth rate in the world.

The 2011-12 budget is based on an average oil price of $55 per barrel and expects to achieve a surplus of QR22.5bn (£3.8bn). Qatar currently has the lowest rate of unemployment in the world and the second highest per-capita income (behind Liechtenstein). Qatar is pressing ahead with ambitious social, economic and infrastructure development plans (together with the expansion of LNG production).

Qatar will invest tens of billions of pounds to develop its infrastructure over the next 10 years or so. Its successful bid to host the World Cup in 2022 provides a real focal point for projects including rail and the New Doha Port. Rapid population growth is driving demand for accommodation (both residential and commercial) and medical and education services. More than 50 new hotels are currently under construction or in the planning stages.

The UK is one of Qatar's key trading partners. The UK exported goods worth £990m to Qatar in 2010 (up 27% on 2009 figures). Exports included industrial machinery and equipment, electrical machinery, vehicles and power generation equipment. The value of the UK's invisible exports including legal, financial and consultancy services was £484m in 2009. Last year Qatar's exports to the UK increased by 205% (from £737m in 2009 to £2,247m in 2010) due increases in the flow of Liquefied Natural Gas (LNG) coming in through the South Hook terminal in

Milford Haven, Wales, which was opened in April 2009 by HH The Emir and HM The Queen. The UK and Qatar have signed a number of agreements and Memorandums of Understanding in recent years, including a Double Taxation Agreement in June 2009. HH The Emir of the State of Qatar, Sheikh Hamad bin Khalifa Al-Thani, accompanied by his Consort HH Sheikha Mozah bint Nasser Al-Missned paid a State Visit to the UK in October 2010. During the visit, a Qatar-UK Memorandum of Understanding on Business, Trade and Technical Cooperation was signed.

Chapter 49: Business Opportunities in Qatar

Qatar's economic diversification and investment in human capital in accordance with the Qatar Vision 2030 continue to generate opportunities for UK businesses across a wide range of sectors. Sectors which offer significant opportunities are:

Construction

The government continues to invest heavily in priority projects including transport, power and water infrastructure. Many private sector projects are also planned or underway, although some have been delayed in the last two years due to the wider global recession. There is increasing interest in green and sustainable building standards, services, products and technologies, as seen for example in the Msheireb heart of Doha redevelopment. Qatar's successful bid to host the FIFA World Cup 2022 will also provide opportunities for construction related work surrounding this event (building and maintenance of sports stadia etc).

Education and Training

Education and training is a key focus of the Qatar Foundation, which is headed by Sheikha Mozah, consort of HH The Emir. The 2400-acre Education City (part of the Qatar Foundation) offers a base for leading international universities wishing to establish a campus presence in Qatar.

Energy Sector

Qatar is investing in research and development programs in the energy sector. Given the local environment/climate, a particular area of interest is solar energy, including its use in water desalination.

Transport

Qatar's three ports in Doha (Qatar's main commercial seaport), Ras Laffan (the world's largest LNG exporting facility) and Mesaieed (Qatar's main oil export terminal and main entry point for aggregates/other building materials) need additional capacity as the economy grows. Construction of the $7bn New Doha Port starts in 2011, with the 1st phase scheduled for completion in 2016 and the whole project due for completion by circa 2030.

Construction of the 1st phase of the New Doha International Airport (NDIA), which will be able to handle 50m passengers, 2m tonnes of cargo and 320,000 aircraft landings and take-offs per year on completion in 2015, is underway. This is the first airport in the world to be custom-built to handle the new A380 aircraft (the largest in the world).

The $4bn Qatar-Bahrain causeway ("Friendship Bridge") was originally to be completed by 2015 but construction has recently stalled. It is hoped that works will recommence soon. Other road projects include the Doha Expressway and the North Road (linking Doha to Al-Khor, Al-Ruwais and finally to Zubarah where it will connect to the causeway to Bahrain). There is also a diverse, state of the art 80 plus station metro system planned for completion by 2026, a high-speed rail link between the NDIA and Doha city centre (which will eventually extend to Bahrain via the causeway) as well as a line to Saudi Arabia and a freight rail link between Ras Laffan and Mesaieed via Doha. The Qatar-Bahrain causeway is envisaged as the start of a Gulf Coast rail link, which (if realised) is to connect Istanbul in Turkey with Muscat in Oman. There are also plans for a rail link on the proposed Doha-Abu Dhabi causeway.

Qatar's Public Works Authority announced in early 2010 that it would launch projects worth $30bn in the next 5 to 8 years. The total amount earmarked for infrastructure is estimated to be between $65-100bn over the next decade.

Sport

At the end of 2010 Qatar was successful in bidding to host the FIFA World Cup 2022. This will undoubtedly provide unparalleled opportunities for foreign companies to work on projects surrounding the competition. In particular, since the UK will be hosting the Olympic Games in London in 2012, there will be a huge amount of potential for British businesses that have worked on the Games to bring the knowledge and experience they have gained there to Qatar. Aside from the World Cup, Qatar has been keen to establish itself as a global sporting destination and, as part of its decade-long modernisation programme; the development of sport in Qatar has enjoyed unfettered government support. Qatar hosts a number of international sporting competitions, including the Qatar ExxonMobil Open and Qatar Total Open tennis competitions, and will be hosting the Arab Games in December 2011. Qatar is also home to ASPIRE – one of the largest indoor sports facilities in the world.

Life Sciences/Healthcare

With its ever-increasing population, Qatar is looking to invest heavily in its life-sciences sector, particularly in healthcare. QR8.8bn (£1.5bn) of the 2011-12 state budget has been earmarked for expansions and improvements within the sector.

Qatar's aim of providing effective domestic healthcare services is coupled with aspirations to become a research and development centre including in the area of life sciences. Through these initiatives Qatar aims to become the healthcare centre of choice for the region. An important element in delivering this will be a new medical and research centre – Sidra.

A growing importance is being attached to in-country after sales services either through the establishment of an office in Qatar or through a reliable agent/distributor. Products are assessed against American standards and leaving free product samples with medical establishments to test has some traction in terms of securing sales. Significant opportunities for Western life science companies in Qatar exist in healthcare investment and operation, provision of hospital furniture, training of medical staff, work around preventative care, pharmaceuticals and medical research.

Defence and Security (Including Fire)

Opportunities in the defence sector are dominated by large companies, especially in aerospace engineering. Due to the vast number of construction and other projects taking place throughout the country, there is a constant need for site security provision. Other opportunities exist in training in the security and fire sectors. Major projects such as road and rail infrastructure (requiring traffic surveillance/violation systems), access control for the ports and railways and security and fire safety for the metro system could also provide opportunities.

Chapter 50: Entering Qatar Market

To succeed in Qatar, foreign businesses must be prepared and able to invest the necessary time, money and effort. The process of establishing a presence in the market can take many months.

Identifying suitable partners, agents or distributors can be time consuming and potentially frustrating. UK businesses need to take a long-term perspective and think in terms of developing partnerships. Businesses that demonstrate a willingness to invest in Qatar and a real commitment to the country are appreciated.

Foreign businesses should do their research before coming to Qatar. They should find out about the organisations and people they are likely to see, try to understand what their objectives are and what they might be looking for. If you are planning to do businesses in Qatar for the first time, you should try to talk to someone who has been there and can provide an insight about what to expect. Above all, it is important to understand that there are many aspects of doing business in Qatar which differ from the UK or USA. What is best practice at home may not be best practice in Qatar.

There are challenges for foreign companies in operating in Qatar. Companies must be prepared to invest the necessary time, money and effort to maximise opportunities for success. The process of registering with local authorities can be difficult. The Qatari Ministry of Business and Trade is keen to implement changes; for example the recent reduction in the rate of tax paid by foreign companies to a flat rate of 10%. A relatively small pool of potential agents or distributors reinforces the need to carefully research and assess the market before entering into any kind of commercial agreement. Although Qatar has started to offer free zone type incentives, such as the Qatar Financial Centre and Education City, free zones as evidenced in other Gulf States do not exist. Very specific criteria apply to the kinds of activities that companies must undertake to qualify for incentives which is part of Qatar's wider strategy to attract only those industries and sectors which complement or add value to existing businesses.

Companies are always advised to seek legal/taxation advice before entering into a joint venture, agency agreement or similar type of partnership.

Getting Paid - Terms of Payment

Irrevocable letters of credit (L/C) and cash against deposit (CAD) are the most common forms of payment.

Responding to Tenders

Most Government purchases over QR50,000 (approx £9,000) are conducted through a tendering process stipulated by the Qatar Central Tender Committee (www.ctc.gov.qa). These tenders will often use standard Terms and Conditions of contract and the use of both Tender Bonds and Performance Bonds is common. Companies may also be required to specify plans to establish a local presence, although this is not so typical for consultancy based contracts, and there is scope for variation clauses to be approved. However, companies seeking to operate a contract from a distance in the UK can be at a disadvantage to competitors who already have a local partner or other form of local presence. Tenders may be "General", "Limited" or "Local", and different rules regarding advertising, applicability to bid and value apply to each, although the majority of tenders are classed as General and advertised to all. Limited tenders (using a shortlist of companies) require the approval of the Minister of Finance prior to bidding and contract award. Local tenders are restricted to a value below QR1,000,000 and use a prior approved shortlist of companies all of whom must be registered with the Chamber of Commerce. Price remains the most important factor in the buying decision with only limited evidence of quality issues being considered and "value based" decision making. That said, UK products enjoy a good reputation in the market. Quotations should be given in Qatari Riyals or $US, and where equipment is concerned, the correct INCOTERM should be researched before quoting. It is useful, but not essential, for commercial correspondence to be in Arabic and English. Companies are advised to refer to the instructions on the Central Tender Committee's website www.ctc.gov.qa in terms of the required documentation.

Chapter 51: Qatar General Overview

Arabic is the official language of Qatar. However, English is widely spoken and is the preferred language for business.

Visas

British nationals can obtain one month visas at immigration on arrival at the airport. They cost around QR100. You will need to pay for your visa with a credit or debit card using a pin number; cash is not accepted.

It is illegal to bring alcohol or pork products into Qatar.

Hotels

At certain times of year it can be very difficult to find a hotel room in Doha. Qatar regularly hosts senior visitors including heads of state and an increasing number of international conferences, seminars and exhibitions. During these times hotel space is at a premium so book your accommodation early.

Hours of Business

Qatar is at GMT+3 and does not use daylight savings. The local weekend is Friday-Saturday. Government ministries and departments operate officially from

0730-1430, Sunday to Thursday. Some local companies work a split shift, generally 0800-1300 and 1600-2000 Saturday to Thursday. During the holy month of Ramadan, working hours will vary.

Getting Around Doha

Getting around Doha can be a challenge. Relatively speaking, it is not a large city but traffic congestion can be heavy. Allow plenty of travel time between appointments. Ensure you have clear, up to date directions as it can be difficult to locate particular buildings or offices. Addresses are usually given as PO boxes, street names are not always clear and locals are accustomed to navigating by landmarks. Finding taxis in some parts of town can be difficult.

Taxi drivers will often not know the place you are looking for; this includes the British Embassy in the 'new' diplomatic area near the 'rainbow roundabout' in the West Bay area of Doha.

Consider hiring a car and driver through your hotel or booking a taxi for the whole day or duration of your visit; these are relatively inexpensive. If you pre-book a taxi it can save money.

Cars with drivers can also be hired from car rental companies including Avis, Budget and Hertz.

Meetings and Presentations

Time is relative; if someone you have arranged to see turns up late for a meeting it does not mean they are not interested in talking to you. You should not be surprised if meetings are interrupted by phone calls, requests for signatures or other points of urgent business. You should be prepared to attend meetings in the evening; much business is done at this time of day.

If it is a first meeting, take a cue from the host; some people prefer to feel comfortable with you before moving on to the real business. Others may be short of time and want to get things done quickly. You should be flexible and not count on delivering a long power-point presentation; hold it in reserve for a follow-up meeting if judged appropriate. Delivery should be kept short, simple and clear. It should not be assumed that the person being addressed speaks fluent English. Turns of phrase and slang may not be well understood.

You should prepare for the meeting by finding out about whom you are seeing and the organisation they represent. You should understand something about the environment you are entering, tread lightly and listen. It is important to take a long-term view of all business relationships; investing time in establishing relationships is key.

Your Pitch

The Qatari market is very competitive. There are many companies here doing business from across the Middle East, UK, US, Europe and Asia. You should not assume everyone you meet will automatically understand that you offer the best product or service.

There are many people knocking on doors here trying to sell themselves. You need to consider the environment in which you are operating, include local case studies and adapt your pitch to best address local needs.

Intellectual Property

IP rights are territorial, that is they only give protection in the countries where they are granted or registered. If you are thinking about trading internationally, then you should consider registering your IP rights in your export markets.

Trademarks can be registered at the Qatar Trade Mark Office. Inventive designs or industrial models can also be registered under the Trade Mark Law.

Qatar copyright law protects original literary and artistic works including computer programmes and databases which are creative in the selection and arrangement of their subject matter - materials must be registered at the Qatar Copyright Office to be protected.

Inventions and foreign patents can be registered at the Qatar Patent Office. However, a GCC Patent can be obtained by filing an application at the Patent Office in Saudi Arabia. Certificates of Patents granted by the GCC Patent Office secure legal protection of the inventor's rights in all member states (UAE, Bahrain, Saudi Arabia, Oman, Qatar and Kuwait).

Chapter 52: Education Sector in Qatar

Qatar is investing significant amounts into education at all levels. The country's hydrocarbon-fuelled economy has provided the means to rapidly develop an evolving education system with the necessary resources by committing a substantial amount of money and brainpower towards providing free, quality education to citizens for decades. The government continues to invest heavily in its efforts to turn its vision into a reality. Education has been allocated QR19.3bn (£3.3bn) in the 2011/12 national budget.

The State education system in Qatar is free at all levels for Qatari citizens. With the establishment of an Independent Schools System, English has become the medium of education.

In order to fulfil the vision of the education leadership the government created the Supreme Education Council (SEC) as part of the first stage of an ongoing restructuring effort and a nationwide initiative known as 'Education for a New Era.' The SEC is responsible for education policy and setting broad and comprehensive goals for the school system. Under SEC, a new school system known as The Independent School Model was introduced. With the introduction of National Community College Project under SEC has become as part of 2030 National Vision. The Community College provides students with post-secondary vocational education and job training that could lead to pursuing a university bachelor's degree or a career in the industry upon graduation.

Education has also become an integral part of the activities of some big companies in Qatar as part of their social responsibility. A major developer, Msheireb Properties, have recently launched 'Green Schools Programme' where schools are encouraged to adopt green best practices. The programme aims to reach, inspire and reward students and schools based on their eco-conscious activities. Doha Bank and UNESCO have also launched a similar programme recently, Eco-Schools Programme, aimed at encouraging and supporting implementation of good environmental practices, reduction of the carbon footprint and increased Eco-consciousness.

Chapter 53: Conclusion

As Qatar invests billions of dollars in infrastructure and public works improvements for the 2022 FIFA World Cup, the country needs partners dedicated to long-term relationships and commitments.

And to do business effectively in the small but wealthy Middle Eastern country, businesses need to have people on the ground that can build strong relationships with Qatari clients. You will not do business in Qatar if you're not there to develop the personal relationships that enable people to get comfortable with you. Comfort, familiarity and trust are more important that the actual bottom-line price.

A land rich in natural gas and oil reserves, Qatar has a gross domestic product per capita that ranks among the best in the world, according to the World Bank, but is looking to diversify its economy.

The Middle Eastern kingdom has placed a strong focus on education and developing a service-based economy, so businesses need to evaluate their investments with an eye toward the long term. The future for that country, in their view, is education and political evolution. Their horizon is the generation beyond the generation now in school.

In partnership with the Qatar Foundation, a semi-public non-profit focused on education and community building, several leading universities have opened campuses in Qatar, including Carnegie Mellon

University, Cornell University and Georgetown University.

The goal of attracting these institutions, open to both male and female students, is to help create a sustainable economy not primary dependent on oil or natural gas exports, according to the Qatar Foundation.

However, in areas like public infrastructure, Qatar remains 20-25 years behind other countries in the region, an issue it hopes to address by hosting the 2022 World Cup.

With plans to build several massive, state-of-the-art stadiums and numerous public works projects, the Qatari government has reportedly set aside $50 billion dollars for construction.

The tournament, which marks the first time a country in the Middle East will host the World Cup, is widely seen as a means for the country to increase its international profile as it seeks to become a larger player in the international community.

A close military ally of the United States and UK, Qatar has also made strong efforts in recent years to engage itself with other Arabic and Middle Eastern countries diplomatically.

However, doing business in a country where friendships with members of the ruling family are often crucial to the success of a deal can be daunting to some investors. To do business in Qatar, it helps to be close to the decision makers, the members of the ruling family. But that's not necessarily a bad thing. Qatar is a country that appreciates technology and is very sophisticated in many regards.

Qatar is not democratic but it is very stable, and it stands out from the other emirates as a progressive, forward looking state open to modernizing its economy.

Largely spared the effects of the Arab Spring uprisings still plaguing other Middle Eastern regimes, most notably in neighbouring Bahrain, the kingdom of Qatar has taken a very slow transition to a more democratic government over the past decade.

Qatar adopted a new constitution in 2003 promising direct elections to the country's limited legislative body, the Majlis al-Shura or Advisory Council, although the emir of the country has postponed them on several occasions.

Good Luck!